Endorsements

Tammie Southerland is a match looking for fuel in a lost and jaded generation. If you get too close, beware, you may just start to burn.

Dean Briggs
Author of *Ekklesia Rising*
Coauthor of *The Jesus Fast* with Lou Engle

A book on fire only comes from a writer on fire. A writer aflame is one who has lingered in the secret place long enough to be consumed by His holy fire. Such a burning one is Tammie Southerland. Just as the Father spoke through a burning bush to Moses, so, too, is the Father's voice thundering through His burning one, Tammie, in this hour. She knows the depths of Father's heart. As such, her words are weighty because she writes from a place of deep consecration before Him—a place of fiery intimacy. For years I've observed a purity in Tammie that sets her apart. I can attest that she has no agenda. She has no ulterior motives but one: For you to personally encounter the fiery heart of the Father as revealed through the face of Christ! *Permission to Burn* will ignite your heart for Him.

Read. Pray. Burn. Then join the ranks of those with burning hearts!

Brian Francis Hume
Servant, writer, intercessor, revivalist
Cofounder of the Breakthrough Tribe

This book will inspire you to come out of a complacent, status-quo life into a radical life on fire. It will provoke you to passionate pursuit of intimacy with God. Your heart will begin to burn as you read it.

Doyle Bradford
Founder of The Father's House International Church
Author of *Journey to Destiny*

Tammie Southerland has been anointed by God to ignite a fire in the hearts of many for pure and simple-hearted devotion to Jesus. This book will stir hunger and holy desire inside your soul for more of Jesus and the Word of God. Tammie is a firebrand, and this manual will be used to call an army of consecrated messengers forth in these last days. Read with expectation. There is more!

Jeremiah Johnson
Founder of Heart of the Father Ministries
Author of *Cleansing and Igniting the Prophetic*

For those of you desiring a deeper fire for the things of God, I highly recommend you read this book. Tammie's passion for Jesus spills out of these pages, so get ready for an impartation and an invitation to *burn* every day for His kingdom!

Jonathan Ngai
Lead minister of Radiance International
CEO Radiance Music Group Visionary, Movement 133

When I met Tammie, I was immediately struck by her pure and humble spirit, but there was a strength and boldness and fire in her eyes that made me want to stand a little closer to her. She is of a new breed of firebrands who will reach the next generation with a steady and solid devotion to know Jesus and make Him known. This book is her story and will convict and provoke you to get breakthrough over your circumstances and then to pick up your sword and advance the kingdom! *Permission to Burn*—yes, indeed!

Mary Kemp
Pastor of New Life Church

Romans 12:11 says, "Never be lacking in zeal, but keep your spiritual fervor, serving the Lord." In my ministry experiences with Tammie Southerland, I have seen that she is a woman who overflows with passion for the Lord. She has exemplified this spiritual fervor, this burning life of zeal for Jesus. If you want to burn with passion and hunger for Jesus, then let this book fan the flames of your heart!

Matthew Lilley
National Director at Burn 24-7 USA

In every generation, God raises up faithful messengers who compel the church to cling hard and live abandoned to the fullness of His divine love. With *Permission to Burn*, Tammie Southerland emerges with a timely exhortation in the lineage and supernatural grace of those who have embraced the crucible of divine preparation amidst the fellowship of the burning ones. Her voice is nuanced with the prophetic, the personal, and the very practical; making this book a critical resource for both mature Christians and brand-new believers.

Jonathan Tremaine Thomas
Founder of Civil Righteousness, Inc.

Permission to Burn

Breaking the chains of compromise from a holy generation

Tammie Southerland

Fire House Publishing

© 2019 by Tammie Southerland
All rights reserved.

This book is protected by the copyright laws of the United States of America. This book may not be copied or reprinted for commercial gain or profit. The use of short quotations or occasional page copying for personal or group study is permitted and encouraged. Permission will be granted upon request. For more information, contact the author at PO Box 1177, Central, SC 29630 or Tammie@frontlinefire.org.

Published 2019
Printed in the United States of America.

Unless otherwise identified, Scripture quotations are taken from the NEW AMERICAN STANDARD BIBLE®, Copyright © 1960,1962,1963,1968,1971,1972,1973,1975,1977,1995 by The Lockman Foundation. Used by permission.

Scripture marked NIV are taken from THE HOLY BIBLE, NEW INTERNATIONAL VERSION®, NIV®. Copyright © 1973, 1978, 1984, 2010 by Biblica, Inc.™ www.xulonpress.com.

The Holy Bible, Berean Study Bible, BSB. Copyright ©2016 by Bible Hub. Used by Permission. All Rights Reserved Worldwide. http://bereanbible.com/

Scripture marked NKJV are taken from the New King James Version. Copyright © 1982 by Thomas Nelson, Inc. Used by permission. All rights reserved.

Scripture quotations marked ESV are taken from The Holy Bible, English Standard Version® (ESV®), copyright © 2001 by Crossway, a publishing ministry of Good News Publishers. Used by permission. All rights reserved.

Scripture quotations marked KJV are taken from the King James Version.

Scripture quotations marked TPT are from The Passion Translation®. Copyright © 2017, 2018 by Passion & Fire Ministries, Inc. Used by permission. All rights reserved. The PassionTranslation.com.

Southerland, Tammie. Permission to Burn: Breaking the chains of compromise from a holy generation

ISBN- 978-1-7334721-0-4 (print)
ISBN- 978-1-7334721-1-1 (eBook)

This book is dedicated to my husband, the FireHouse staff, my biological and spiritual children, and to the next generation of firebrands. Without you, this work is in vain. You are the pieces to this puzzle and the arrows in the quiver of the Lord to be shot out into the nations.

Contents

Foreword i
Introduction iii
Preface vii

1 Shattered Dreams 1
2 Burning Hearts Collide 9
3 The Character of Jesus 25
4 Relationship That Knows No Bounds ... 35
5 Love-Sick Warriors 51
6 Holy Dissatisfaction 63
7 Purification and Offense 73
8 The Dream of Kingdom Unity 85
9 Permission to Go 101
10 The Marriage of Wisdom and Zeal 117
11 Living as Sons and Daughters 127
12 Dreaming Heaven's Dreams 143
13 Birthing the Bride 149
14 From Permission to Ascension 171

Appendix A 185
Appendix B 187

About Tammie 191

Foreword

In Luke 12:49, Jesus declares, "I have come to cast fire upon the earth; and how I wish it were already kindled!" One of the primary missions of Jesus's coming was to start a holy fire that would fill the whole earth. It was this vision that drove Him through the cross, up from the dead, and ultimately into heaven, so He could pour out His Spirit, fill the earth, and beckon His return.

I believe we are moving into the days that will culminate with the literal return of Jesus Christ, and these will be days of fire. God is raising up leaders, like Tammie Southerland, who won't try to quench or control the fire, but who will give a generation permission to burn all their days—with anointed works and deep intimacy with the Holy Spirit.

In this book, Permission to Burn, Tammie sounds a call for a generation of people who won't be content to live on the edges of Christianity but who will want to throw themselves into the radical lifestyle of prayer, fasting, and proclamation of the burning Man Himself, Jesus Christ. God is raising up a breed of believers who aren't just looking for what they can get away with and stay saved, but who are asking a different set of questions, like, "How far will You let me go, and how abandoned will You let me be?" If you are ready to be provoked into a deeper place in your walk with God, then this book is for you.

Corey Russell
Author of *The Glory Within* and *Ancient Paths*

Introduction

While the company of burning ones is being made ready for the work of the Lord, God always uses the times of trial. No detail escapes the eyes of the Lord. Times of repugnant darkness are but a means for the Lord to raise up sons and daughters who burn for the light of His glory to be unveiled in the coming hour. The repulsive stench of crippling darkness sets the stage for a showdown, as the hidden ones proclaim in secret before the Lord that the darkness will not overcome the light of the glory of Christ Jesus. (see John 1:5).

These hidden ones burn for the fame of His glorious splendor to be made known through their lives. Their greatest legacy? A burning heart that is fueled by the fiery love of the Godhead to run in the paths of the greatest commandment (see Matt. 22:36-40). Burning hearts do not permit compromise to settle within. When roots of idolatry do sprout within the lives of burning ones, inaction does not rule the moment. Instead repentance quickly uproots such compromise. This process of repentance is attained through godly sorrow as sons and daughters are "transformed by the renewal of [their] mind" (Rom. 12:2 ESV). Such tilling within the soil of burning hearts cultivates pliable ones in the hands of the Father.

Tammie Southerland demonstrates this reality in her life. Years ago, while attending Christ for the Nations Institute in Dallas, Texas, I read a book by Ronnie Floyd aptly titled *Life on Fire*. Recently, while preparing a message on this very topic, I pulled the book off my bookshelf. As I opened *Life on Fire*, I was riveted by one sentence in an endorsement by Dale Schlafer. It gripped me. I paused as I stared intently at seven words: "Some authors write better than they live."

My response? No, I did not want to be one who wrote better than he lived. Nor one who preached better than he lived. I can assure you that Tammie, the author of *Permission to Burn*, wrote from a depth of revelation that only a burning heart can seize. This book was wrought forth in secret in the crucible of the Father's fierce testing. You will capture a glimpse into Tammie's honest struggles. You will walk through the crucible with Tammie as her story mirrors aspects of your own heart journey with the Lord. As you continue to read the book, you will invariably experience the crucible of His refining, fiery love. Each chapter will introduce you to biblical principles that were experienced firsthand by Tammie as she encountered the depths of the Father's love. Tammie possessed a burning heart before one word was ever written in this manuscript. What you hold in your hands today was first lived out within the heart of a fiery one in the secret place.

Permission to Burn is a remarkably anointed book. Prophetically speaking, I hear the Lord saying that this book is a gift to the bride of Christ that will keep on giving for the decades to come. Many will come into their calling as burning ones, which will empower them to leave behind a glorious legacy unto the Lord. The legacy of a burning heart is boundlessly potent in the hands of God. Through the orchestration of the Holy Spirit, this book will ignite a generation of burning hearts.

Permission to Burn will find itself in the boardrooms of Fortune 500 companies and on nightstands in bedrooms; in palaces of rulers spawned across the Middle East and Asia; in dorm rooms of university students across the globe. It will be read by passengers crisscrossing the nations of the earth on airplanes, boats, and trains. But, most importantly, it will reach into the hearts ready to burn for Jesus Christ. Many, like John Wesley of old, will utter, "I felt my heart strangely warmed," as they trust Christ alone for saving faith that galvanizes into a movement of burning hearts. Countless lives will encounter the fiery love of the Holy One within the pages of this combustible book.

Before you proceed with the first chapter, I want to ask you a few simple questions.

> Are you born again?
> Is there known compromise in your life?
> Is there any darkness that has captivated your affections?
> Do you long for Him above all else this world has to offer?
> Has the baptism of fire so consumed you that you burn inwardly alone for Him?
> Are you ablaze with the same fiery love Jesus experiences eternally within the Godhead?

The pervading darkness of the times is but an invitation to become a part of the company of burning ones. In other words, permission to burn is issued from the Father to all regardless of where you are in life. In due time burning hearts emerge from the crucible, those who have withstood the test of time in secret. Such an example of this is recorded in the Scriptures. Israel the nation was steeped in darkness due to the idolatry of King Ahab and his diabolical wife Jezebel.

Dark, dark clouds blinded a nation when suddenly a burning one appeared. Elijah the Tishbite emerged unannounced, a grown man (1 Kings 17:1), but more importantly, a prophet ablaze in the hands of God.

Nothing is known of his previous life. Without question he was a man called to shape the times. Elijah was a prophet summoned to confront gross darkness. Though "Elijah was a man just like us" (James 5:17 BSB), God used this burning one to turn the tide of idolatry in a nation.

Remember, the Lord has "determined allotted periods and the boundaries of their dwelling place," meaning: the location and timing of your birth was no mistake! (Acts 17:26 ESV). You were born for "such a time as this" (Esther 4:14). There is no other time period that you are better suited for than right now, at this precise moment. Simply stated: You were born to burn!

As you read *Permission to Burn* from cover to cover, may you declare from the depths of your being, "I was born to burn for you, Jesus!"

Brian Francis Hume
Burning for Him
December 2018

Preface

Rid yourselves, therefore, of all malice, deceit, hypocrisy, envy, and slander. Like newborn infants, crave pure spiritual milk, so that by it you may grow up in your salvation, now that you have tasted that the Lord is good.

As you come to Him, the living stone, rejected by men, but chosen and precious in God's sight, you also, like living stones, are being built into a spiritual house to be a holy priesthood, offering spiritual sacrifices acceptable to God through Jesus Christ. For it stands in Scripture:

> "See, I lay in Zion a stone,
>> a chosen and precious cornerstone;
> and the one who believes in Him
>> will never be put to shame."

To you who believe, then, this stone is precious. But to those who do not believe,

> "The stone the builders rejected
>> has become the cornerstone,"

and,

> "A stone of stumbling
>> and a rock of offense."

They stumble because they disobey the word—and to this they were appointed.

But you are a chosen people, a royal priesthood, a holy nation, a people for God's own possession, to proclaim the virtues of Him who called you out of darkness into His marvelous light. Once you were not a people, but now you are the people of God; once you had not received mercy, but now you have received mercy.

Permission to Burn

> Beloved, I urge you, as foreigners and exiles, to abstain from the desires of the flesh, which war against your soul. Conduct yourselves with such honor among the Gentiles that, though they slander you as evildoers, they may see your good deeds and glorify God on the day He visits us.
>
> – 1 Peter 2:6-12 BSB

Now, therefore, may the chains of compromise be broken as you read these words and step into your identity as part of a holy generation!

David said it this way:

> Now, my son, the Lord be with you, and may you have success and build the house of the Lord your God, as he said you would. May the Lord give you discretion and understanding when he puts you in command . . . so that you may keep the law of the Lord your God. Then you will have success . . . I have taken great pains to provide for the temple of the Lord . . . and you may add to [these provisions]. You have many workers: . . . the Lord be with you.
>
> – 1 Chronicles 22:11-16, NIV

My heart's cry is that you take these words, which is the heart of the Lord, and make it your life to burn with passion for Him. May the Lamb receive the reward of His suffering.

Tammie Southerland

1
SHATTERED DREAMS

I'm eight years old. Another dollar drops into an old shoebox. One more dollar toward my independence. Laugh if you want, I would say in my mind, but I will own a two-story home on the beach. I am going to change the world.

Ten years old. I am walking into the local mall with my head held high. There is a huge display of art and short stories written by children from all over the state. I am overwhelmed with joy, as I am about to be honored as the number-one child author and illustrator in the state of South Carolina. The Young Authors Award is placed in my hand and my mother swells with pride.

At the age of fourteen, I've fallen in love with Jesus and dream of traveling the world one day with my husband and our four children.

Permission to Burn

I have always been an old soul and a limitless dreamer. From a very young age, I believed I was more mentally and spiritually mature than my peers. Independence is part of my nature. I was an unconventional child and a self-reliant teenager. Going into college, I just knew I was going to be a maverick adult.

I was ready to take over the world. I had dreams. I had longings. I had a plan. I even had plans of marrying and starting a family with my high school sweetheart. I was the tender age of seventeen. But we had compromised our purity. I was grieved deeply, as I had made a commitment to God to stay sexually pure until marriage. For two teenagers, years of dating feels like a lifetime. We were one another's first serious relationship—first everything. We thought we had the perfect solution to fix the mistake of compromising.

He took me to the lake, made a beautiful dinner, and asked me to marry him. Marriage would make it all perfect, right? Wrong! It wasn't long until we realized that the ring and wedding wouldn't fix the deeper, yet unspoken, problem. A shouting match erupted "No! I do not want to sleep together again until we get married. I made a commitment to God of purity. Compromising sexual purity crushes God's heart. Engagement is not marriage. Let's take a respite from one another and seek God's will," I yelled. To my surprise, he responded in agreement to a pause in our engagement. Like a train coming to a halt, I discovered that my exciting safe zone wasn't as safe as I'd thought.

I was very naïve in my maturity and independence. I was crushed in spirit, but I had gained new friends since entering college, so I agreed to go out with them to a frat party and hang out.

Soon, another fight would take place when I ran to my high school sweetheart for help. In my mind, we were on a break, but I just knew that he would stand with me, no matter what. He was not just a boyfriend; he was my best friend. Then he said something that shocked me. "I will not let your rape get us back together." He walked away. I felt alone and immensely confused. Where was God in all of this? What was happening? Confusing thoughts raced through my mind. It was as if the world were whirling around me in slow motion. My heart, dreams, and identity crashed to the floor and shattered into a million pieces.

Early into my college career, I found out what sexual abuse is and what it means to be subdued, pushed down, and silenced. I discovered what it was like to lose my identity as a strong, powerful young woman and to become an abused, submissive, binge-drinking mess. I went to college on fire, ready to take over the world. Within months, after pledging a sorority, I found myself confused and wounded. Not only had my relationship with my fiancé ended, but I was also drugged and raped at the party that night. I was spiritually, mentally, emotionally, and physically traumatized. I found myself in situation after situation where I didn't have a voice. I lived in fear, and I repeatedly found myself in situations where men took advantage of me. Before I knew it, even though I was trying to pull myself out of this pit, I ended up being deceived by a fellow student into a trafficking situation.

Events like these silence and enslave a person, pouring water on the fire inside. Events like these scream *You have no voice! You have no rights! You're just an item to be used.* After walking through so much hell, I was desperate for a way out.

Permission to Burn

I am an all-or-nothing type of person. Growing up, I had attended a church where we just sat in our pews. It was a sweet little country church, but I experienced no power behind what I believed. As I walked through this trauma, I realized this kind of traditional church attendance was not working to heal my shattered life. I couldn't just sit in the church pew, because I didn't feel clean enough. I felt dirty and shameful. I had made choices I had never thought possible. I had forgotten the love God had for me. I had entered college with a vision, a plan, and academic focus, yet I found myself standing in the middle of a whirlwind, looking in the mirror and having no idea who I was anymore.

The people who surrounded me in college continually silenced me, telling me that if I spoke of any of it, they would make my life a living hell. This trauma on top of trauma happened for a solid year. For me, it was enough to squelch my identity—that fireball, that independent woman, that child with a vision who believed her daddy when he said, "You can do anything if you put your mind to it." I couldn't put my mind to anything anymore. The only thing consuming my mind was my own worthlessness. Damaged goods. Unworthy of any help.

During the summer after my freshman year, I frequented bars and partied like I didn't care if I lived or died. One night, my younger brother came to the bar, grabbed a beer, and looked at me. "What is going on with you?" he asked.

"You have no idea what I've been through," I said. "And I don't want to talk about it. You don't need to be doing what I'm doing. Go home!"

Before I knew it, more of his friends from our local youth group came into the bar. *What are these people doing?*

Don't get involved in what I'm doing, I thought. *Go home and be good ol' boys.*

That night turned into a night of drinking, partying, and brokenheartedness. In the wee hours of the morning, after we were both completely drunk, my brother looked at me and said, "I want you to go on a youth retreat with me tomorrow."

Is he crazy? I wondered. I could think of many reasons why I should not go. *He's drunk, I'm drunk. We can't go on a Baptist youth retreat with a hangover. What we are doing is utter sin.* No one knew what I'd been through, and the last thing I wanted was to be around people who were going to judge me. I was only a shell of a person.

Desperate

When I returned to my apartment early that morning, I picked up my Bible in my arms, along with a cross I had made as a child, and I cried out to God, "If You will get me out of this, I will give my entire life to You! I don't know how to get out. God, forgive me, forgive me, forgive me! Take away this feeling! Take away this sickness! Get me out of this!" I didn't bother to shower or change clothes. I cried until I passed out on the bed with my Bible in my arms.

I woke up a few hours later, strangely compelled to drive to my hometown, get on that bus if they would let me, and go on that youth retreat. I figured if all the drunks who were out with me the night before were on that retreat, they couldn't judge me too much. I pulled into the parking lot of Siloam Baptist Church, and there they all were—about to pull out of the parking lot. Miss Lynn Sargent—who loved me dearly, had known me since I was a little girl, and had prayed for me like I was her own—

spotted my car pulling into the parking lot and cried, "Stop the bus!" I jumped out of my car with a grocery bag of clothes and asked, "Will you let me go?"

When I got on that church bus, Miss Lynn cried and hugged me, saying, "We missed you! We missed you so much, Tambo!"

All the way there, I thought, *What am I doing? I'm with a bunch of youth who are younger than me. These people have no idea I'm not the same person I used to be. I'm only a shell of that person.* We finally arrived at our beach cabin destination and settled in. Several of us formulated plans to sneak out and go partying later that night, but I felt so much conviction about taking advantage of Miss Lynn.

To begin the retreat, the leaders called everyone to sit on the floor in a circle in the large, sunken living room. I held back and sat on the steps that led into the living room, off in the corner—alone. The youth leaders began sharing their testimonies, but I didn't pay close attention. I felt so ashamed. I didn't know if I should put on my fake face and pretend to be the old Tammie or if I should just be the Tammie trauma had made me. As I wrestled internally, my brother came and sat down beside me. All of a sudden, I heard words from the leader's mouth that broke through my inner conversation. "We used to do drugs."

I immediately turned my head in surprise. *What? They used to do drugs?* My mind began to run an inventory of the things I had done and make a comparison. *I hadn't done drugs. I had been drinking, and many horrible things had happened to me. They used to do drugs, but now they have a beautiful family, and God still loves them?* Suddenly, the power and presence of God fell on me, and I remembered a time when I was in middle school, when I went to a youth camp and was baptized in the Holy Spirit and fire. The people at that youth camp had spoken a prophetic word over me, and though I couldn't remember the word, I remembered the feeling of the presence of God that filled me at that moment. The touch of His Spirit caused beautiful memories to flood my mind. I remembered the burning of my heart for His and His for mine. Now, all these years later, I felt so overwhelmed with this familiar feeling of the power of His presence. I began to weep, and I heard the Lord say, *I love you. I was there. I believe you.*

The Spirit of God caused my face to turn, and I looked at my brother while God continued speaking, *That's what love looks like. I sent him into the darkness to pull you out!* In that moment, I began to understand the love of Jesus that reaches into the darkest places of the human heart, washes away sin, and heals trauma.

No one needed to ask me to say a sinner's prayer. I simply began to pray, "Oh, God! Forgive me! Wash me clean. I don't ever want to go back. Thank You, Lord!" As God wiped my slate clean, I realized I never again wanted that slate to have anything written on it that did not glorify the One who loves me and is with me.

While I was on my knees in the presence of God, weeping and repenting in my heart of hearts, I noticed tears streaming down my brother's face. Within moments, the Spirit of God fell on the entire room, person by person, in our little Baptist youth meeting. Like dominoes, one person after another began weeping and repenting and giving their lives to Jesus.

Most of us had been planning on going through the motions to just "do church," because that was how we had grown up. Most of us had been drunk at the bar the night before, and we had plans to go out and party later that night, when no one was looking. The presence of God demolished our plans. In a moment, our plans became His plans. Our hearts began to burn. In a moment, He showed up, and the entire room of young people wept and repented, giving their lives to Him.

That night, I experienced authentic, transforming revival for the first time in my life, and from then on, I was hooked on His presence. We stood up from that place in absolute awe and wonder at what had happened. At the same time, we knew the sovereign hand of God had poured out His Spirit upon every one of the kids and adults in the room that night, causing a spontaneous repentance and filling of His Spirit. We spent the rest of the night praying, talking, and ministering to one another. The rest of that youth retreat was all about Him. Lives were drastically changed. My brother and I were baptized together, and we said we would run after Jesus the rest of our lives. That was just the beginning.

Has trauma gripped your life? Have you compromised your purity? Do you feel the gripping presence of the Lord? Pray! You don't have to use eloquent words.

CRY OUT

> Oh, Jesus, thank You for Your blood. It washes away the mistakes I have made. I believe! Wash me clean and make me new. Forgive me and empower me by Your Holy Spirit to never go back. Help me to forgive those who hurt me. I want my heart to burn for You!

2
Burning Hearts Collide

Then their eyes were opened and they recognized Him; and He vanished from their sight. They said to one another, "Were not our hearts burning within us while He was speaking to us on the road, while He was explaining the Scriptures to us?" And they got up that very hour and returned to Jerusalem, and found gathered together the eleven and those who were with them. – Luke 24:31–33.

Permission to Burn

The disciples on the road to Emmaus were broken and traumatized. They didn't understand why Jesus had died. The shame and ridicule of being His followers was intense to endure. We can practically hear their thoughts as we read the story in Luke 24. They wondered, *We thought Jesus was our Messiah, and now He's gone–dead. What do we do now? There's nowhere to go.* So they gave up and went back to their old lives as fishermen. But then, there He was—Jesus in His glorified body. Yet they had no idea who He was. He asked them what was bothering them, and in amazement, as though this stranger lived under a rock, they asked, "Do you not know?"

He continued to talk with the brokenhearted disciples for a while, explaining the Scriptures to them; after which He disappeared. The disciples looked at one another and recognized that deep, inner burning in their hearts, and they said, "Oh! It was Him! It was Him!"

How did they know?

Their hearts burned within them as He spoke the truth. All of a sudden, they experienced the fellowship of the burning hearts. And in that place of intimacy and revelation, even in their brokenness, Jesus came. Jesus showed up in His glorified body, but because of their overwhelming emotions, they didn't recognize Him. They were focused on earthly things instead of heavenly things. Instead of rebuking them, Jesus came into their brokenness and encountered them in His glorified body, causing their hearts to burn. Suddenly, they began to remember what it was like to be with Him. They knew it had to be Him.

This is how I encountered the Lord in my brokenness. He came to me. He walked with me down the road of confusion and piercing pain. He spoke truth to me in the darkest of nights. It was a sudden moment when He

BURNING HEARTS COLLIDE

opened my eyes with a revelation of His reckless love and caused my heart to burn again.

According to The Passion Translation, the Aramaic word for "love" literally means "to burn with passion." The disciples knew they had been with Him because of the physical, emotional, and spiritual burning that continued even after He vanished. This burning-heart phenomenon also happened to the prophets of old, like David, Moses, Isaiah, and Jeremiah. David's heart burned with passion for the Lord (Ps. 39:3). He desired one thing and was called a "man after God's own heart" (Ps. 27:4; Acts 13:22). Moses talked to God face to face and breath to breath (Ex. 33:11, 18; Num. 12:8). Isaiah's fiery encounter with the coal to his lips transformed him from being fearful and timid to bold and fearless (Is. 6:6-13). Jeremiah had fire in his heart and bones that compelled him to be true to his commission, even if it meant death (Jer. 20:9). But to these disciples, this was an awakening to the deep inner witness and recognition of the One with whom they were walking—the Christ.

They were also awakened to their identity as the burning ones. A dramatic shift had taken place. In the days of old, only the selected ones experienced the blazing fire of God. Now, Jesus gives a new promise of burning for all. This is how it should be for all who encounter Him—not just at the moment of conversion, but for all of eternity. This reality is the lifestyle of burning that He has won for us.

BORN OF LOVE

I went down into waters of baptism one summer Sunday morning. I didn't take it lightly. It was a day of grand celebration in our little town. Together, my brother and I made a public declaration of our new life in Christ. I remember the feeling of going down and the water rushing over my face. It was as if the old Tammie died in the water that day. I came back up, knowing my past had been washed away. I felt alive, clean, and made new. But the water alone did not cleanse me. The new birth is not one of water only, as Jesus told Nicodemus.

Nicodemus was a religious man and familiar with full submersion in water for the purposes of ceremonial cleansing. Jesus wanted to use this knowledge to help Nicodemus understand that the ritual of outward washing wasn't enough to enter the kingdom of heaven. In the new birth, believers are born of both water and Spirit (see John 3:5). It's a birth of more exceptional promise. As Paul said, "The old things passed away; behold, new things have come" (2 Cor. 5:17). This new life or new birth is a burst of burning in the heart, soul, and spirit, enabling us to fulfil the greatest commandment: "Love the Lord your God with all your heart and with all your soul and with all your strength and with all your mind" (Luke 10:27 NIV). From this place, we will be able to obey the second command: "Love your neighbor as yourself" (Mark 12:31).

John the Baptist, when speaking of Jesus, declared the difference between the baptism of water and the spiritual burning of the baptism of fire. He said, "He who is coming after me is mightier than I, and I am not fit to remove His sandals; He will baptize you with the Holy Spirit and fire" (Matt. 3:11). Jesus spoke of a spiritual birth. John spoke of spiritual baptism. They both pointed to a love that is an unquenchable flame of passion.

In the same way, the Song of Solomon speaks of relentless, burning love that should not be awakened until it so desires, because this fiery love is stronger than death

Burning Hearts Collide

and even more powerful than the grave (see Song 8:4, 6-7). The Song of Solomon talks about this love being a love that is jealous for us—the jealous love of a bridegroom for His bride. We are awakened and born again into a place of burning in our hearts with unquenchable passion. This mix of unquenchable passion and burning love is the very essence of God, who created us in His likeness.

The passion of Jesus on the cross—giving His life for us—is His radical, fiery gift to humanity. John the Baptist declared in Matthew 3:11 that Jesus is the true baptizer, the one who can release a new birth within—a spiritual rebirth by the power of the Holy Spirit that causes an inward blazing-heart phenomenon. Jesus laying down His life and giving us the very Spirit of God is the true manifestation of the love of God. He gave all so that we may understand what it is to know burning desire. He loves us radically and unashamedly, holding nothing back but giving all with a zealous and bleeding heart. This radical, passionate love is the simple gospel.

The disciples, later called apostles, would give their lives for the One they recognized by the burning of their hearts and not merely the sight of their eyes. They would give their lives for the One who gave His life for them. They would find something—someone—greater than the temporal pleasures of the earth. He would become their pleasure and delight, a love worth dying for. When they no longer saw Him in physical form, their hearts were awakened. When we encounter Him, we come alive with an eternal vision that Christ would be known in a tangible way. This is the good news of the gospel.

Jesus said, "You are My friends if you do what I command you. No longer do I call you slaves, for the slave does not know what his master is doing; but I have called you friends, for all things that I have heard from My Father I have made known to you" (John 15:14-15). With a burning heart, He calls us His friends. He went on to say, "You did not choose Me but I chose you, and appointed you that you would go and bear fruit, and that your fruit would remain, so that whatever you ask of the Father in My name He may give to you" (v. 16).

The gospel is a passionate story of our Savior's love for His family. He desperately longs to be with us for all of eternity. Paul said, "How beautiful are the feet of those who bring good news of good things!" (Rom. 10:15). Truly, the gospel is good news—not merely a cerebral or mental awakening, but an awakening of our entire beings to recognize true love. God's love is the embodiment of the burning of His heart of relentless passion toward us. Love is not a thought, feeling, or ideal. Love is not a mere emotion. Love is a person, and this person is named Jesus.

The apostle John made this clear when he wrote,

> Beloved, let us love one another, for love is from God; and everyone who loves is born of God and knows God. The one who does not love does not know God, for God is love. By this the love of God was manifested in us, that God has sent His only begotten Son into the world so that we might live through Him. . . . We have come to know and have believe the love which God has for us. God is love, and the one who abides in love abides in God, and God abides in him.
>
> – 1 John 4:7-9,16

If God is love, it means love is His nature and identity. This God who is love is a person, not a thought or feeling. This should be an awakening to those who call themselves

His. To burn with His love is to burn with the unquenchable fire of that love, regardless of circumstances. The lifestyle of being on fire for God is not for the select few who are extreme; in fact, radical Christianity is not radical at all. It's biblical! To burn for Jesus is not a special calling for a few crazy folks, it's for all who will come.

Not long into my journey of making Jesus my Lord, I found fellowship with other college students who were on fire for Jesus, baptized in His Spirit, and deeply hungry and tenacious for His presence. It was like nothing I'd ever seen. They took me to meetings where people were dancing and worshipping and speaking the Word of God as though it had authority and power. I saw people healed. I saw them burning with God's fire; they truly loved me, and they truly loved Him. The parents of one of these students ministered to me and walked me through inner healing. In the place of God's presence, I began to discover family—true, authentic spiritual family. In this environment, I, too, caught the fire, and I was transformed.

A few year ago, Paul McRae, a worship pastor and close friend, shared a glimpse into his moment of transformation, as his willing heart and the fire of God's love collided.

> My testimonial process began, as in most cases, with full-on repentance. I recall pulling up to the park and witnessing a cloud of Jesus freaks—prophetic dancers, heaven-opening worshippers, and Holy Ghost fire prophets, evangelists, and apostles—really the church and how it should be (the fivefold ministry working in a symphony orchestrated by the Creator Himself). As we all sat there in a circle, prostrate before God, God told

me the idols I was to cast down. Immediately and instantly, the chains were broken. It sounds rather insignificant, but in that moment, I gave up all electronic games (some that I'd been arguably addicted to for four or more years), and basically all media idols I was putting before God for so long. A new realm of freedom has followed me ever since.

After repentance, full-on encounters with Jesus surely followed—from worship sessions out in the barn with some mighty men and women of God, park worship sessions that literally broke the atmosphere and shook hell to its core, to experiencing another level of the Father's love in what the team and I now call The Father's Love Session. Each one exponentially ignited and fueled a flame that had simply been dormant for so long. Now, I cannot get enough of Jesus. I can only move to the sound of His heartbeat. All I strive for is His kingdom and that it would manifest here on earth as it is in heaven.

This is the essence of true salvation—of the new birth in Christ, in which one is born of the Spirit. This salvation restores the ability to live in spiritual communion with God. Adam and Eve shared that kind of intimacy with God in the garden of Eden before they fell into sin. Sin separates, but the love of God restores.

After Jesus was resurrected and appeared to His disciples, He gave them His Spirit, just as He had promised them (John 7:39). We see the fulfillment of His promise in John 20:21-22. "So Jesus said to them again, 'Peace be with you; as the Father has sent Me, I also send you.' And when He had said this, He breathed on them and said to them, 'Receive the Holy Spirit.'"

In the same way that the Father breathed the breath of life into Adam to make him a living soul (in Genesis), so, too, Jesus breathed the *ruach hakodesh*, or Holy Spirit, into His disciples so they might live fully. This is the redemptive, divine reconnect between humanity and God that took place when Jesus shed His blood for the forgiveness of sin. Sin needed to be forgiven so that people could once again live forever as eternal spiritual beings. As the apostle Paul wrote, "For the wages of sin is death, but the free gift of God is eternal life in Christ Jesus our Lord" (Rom. 6:23).

Despite the devil's vile mission, God used sin and death to open the way for the indwelling of His breath, or Spirit, within His sons and daughters again. This passionate impartation is the divine moment John the Baptist spoke about and gave his life for, the great joy set before Jesus that He died and was resurrected for, This moment with His disciples is a taste-and-see moment illustrating what God would soon do, not just for the biblical disciples, but for all who would receive. This soon-to-be fulfillment of Joel's prophecy and promise of the Father would change humanity forever (see Joel 2:28-29). This would enable *all* people to live the lifestyle of burning they were created for. We know we need to be clean, and when we pray from the depths of our soul, He washes our slates and empowers us to pursue a lifestyle of sustained revival.

The apostle Peter described this process.

> "Repent and be baptized, every one of you, in the name of Jesus Christ for the forgiveness of your sins. And you will receive the gift of the Holy

Permission to Burn

> Spirit. The promise is for you and your children and for all who are far off—for all whom the Lord our God will call." With many other words he warned them; and he pleaded with them, "Save yourselves from this corrupt generation."
>
> – Acts 2:38-40 NIV

In this passage, Peter spoke of God's life-giving breath, boldly proclaiming the baptism of the Holy Spirit and salvation of Jesus Christ for all who believe. Peter was overwhelmed with a burning heart full of the Holy Spirit and fire. If we look at Peter's life, we can see a dramatic shift from before Jesus breathed on Peter and filled him with the Spirit and after the outpouring of the Spirit. Peter's boldness and radical life were marked by the breath of God and his burning heart. Before he received the Spirit, Peter denied Christ. After he received the Spirit, Peter gave his life for Christ. History tells us Peter died as a martyr by being hung upside-down on a cross—all for the cause of Christ.

Fire in Our DNA

All the first-century apostles, prophets, evangelists, and other disciples who were marked by Jesus with holy fire were willing to give their lives for Jesus. This is the radical nature of the salvation experience. In my own life, from the moment of repentance on, I experienced an ongoing encounter of this inward fire, or inward baptism, in which I didn't want to do anything but worship. I didn't want to do anything but be with Jesus. I wanted to study and read His Word constantly. I wanted to fellowship with those who were burning like me. It wasn't long before I started taking Bible classes and immersed myself in forty days of prayer at my new church. We would come and pray before going to class. My life drastically changed. I went from partying all night and then trying to go to class to praying all night and then burning when I went to class. I was in love.

This burning passion was also experienced in the Old Testament, through the grace of God, by prophets such as Jeremiah, Isaiah, and Ezekiel. Also, King David, a man after God's own heart, wrote about the burning heart: "My heart was hot within me, while I was musing the fire burned; then I spoke with my tongue" (Ps. 39:3).

The Spirit of burning and hungering for Jesus is available for each one of us. It's the true mark of our salvation. Our calling in God is greater than sitting in a church pew on Sunday morning. It's greater than our fellowship parties. The call of God is great, and it fills us with a passion to know Him and to be known by Him. When we are awakened to this reality, nothing can stop the love of God from burning in and through our veins.

It is a supernatural passion and inward fire, not only a mental understanding of the Scriptures. Through it, the Word of God is infused into our DNA and written on our hearts with the burning passion of God. Paul said it this way:

> In all these things we overwhelmingly conquer through Him who loved us. For I am convinced that neither death, nor life, nor angels, nor principalities, nor things present, nor things to come, nor powers, nor height, nor depth, nor any other created thing, will be able to separate us from the love of God, which is in Christ Jesus our Lord.
> – Romans 8:37-39

Permission to Burn

When the love of God is infused into our DNA, we begin to realize that *absolutely nothing* can put out His love for us nor separate us from Him. We can choose to rebel against Him or renounce Him, but why would we? The fruit of the Matthew 3:11 Holy Spirit-and-fire type of burning love is a seal upon our hearts. This love, the same passion that caused Jesus to lay down His life for us, is supernaturally awakened in us and becomes our very reason for living. Once transformed, we begin to realize that compassion is not just for God but also to be shared with other people. That is the magnificence of the awakening of a burning heart.

Over the years, I have received prayers and blessings—from many people—saying that God will use me in a mighty way for mass harvest and salvations. For a season, I struggled with these blessings, prayers, and prophetic words. I couldn't understand why I wrestled with these words, since the desire of my heart is to see every nation, tribe, and tongue saved. I've now realized that in the depths of my soul, I yearn for something greater than people just coming to say a prayer at the altar in an emotional moment. I long for the altar experience to alter their lives radically and biblically, for all of eternity. I want to see hearts on fire for Him that will never burn out and never be quenched, even in the face of persecution and rejection. I want to see those who will burn hotter when faced with trials.

So I began to cry out to God that if He was going to fill stadiums and auditoriums through me, then I wanted the people who filled those places to not merely follow the crowd in an emotional moment, reciting a sinner's prayer, but to give their lives, knowing the cost, to the cause of Christ. I began to ask God,

> If You are going to do these things through my life, would You somehow cause those who come in to burn with unquenchable fire for You? Please move among my generation and generations to come with an outpouring of Your Spirit and fire, and with true awakening of the heart to love You and to love others in the way You have loved us. Jesus, walk in the mass gatherings and baptize in Holy Spirit fire. Fame, dynamic personality, or persuasive words is not my desire. My one desire is You. I want Your name and Your fame to be great and to be heard in every ear and awaken every heart all over the earth. Jesus, I want a generation to be on fire for You!

Even as I write these words, I weep for you to truly *know* Him in your heart and to burn for Him in the way the apostles and prophets of Scripture did—those who gave their lives for love. Consider these greats of faith.

> Women received back their dead by resurrection; and others were tortured, not accepting their release, so that they might obtain a better resurrection; and others experienced mockings and scourgings, yes, also chains and imprisonment.
>
> They were stoned, they were sawn in two, they were tempted, they were put to death with the sword; they went about in sheepskins, in goatskins, being destitute, afflicted, ill-treated (men of whom the world was not worthy), wandering in deserts and mountains and caves and holes in the ground. And all these, having gained approval through their faith, did not receive what was promised, because

> God had provided something better for us, so that apart from us they would not be made perfect.
> – Hebrews 11:35-40

Like these faithful ones, we can be gripped with His love in a way that is not in vain. May we not love this life so much that we refuse to take their batons in this race to finish manifesting God's glory in the earth.

Would you pray and agree for God to do whatever He needs to do in your life for you to be truly saved, delivered, healed, and set free by the power of His Spirit? Would you agree with me that every false doctrine, and every hindrance of every generation past, would be broken in your mind and heart right now, so that you can receive the truth? Would you agree with me now for the very essence of Jesus to be manifest in your being?

I started this book with the story of a girl who felt empowered and independent but then found herself subdued, silenced, broken, and voiceless. The moment my heart began to burn again, my voice began to return. When I opened my Bible and read, it was like it was brand new all over again. Every single word was like a shaft of light directly from heaven. I believed every word, and I longed to do what it said. I wanted to heal the sick, raise the dead, prophesy, dream dreams, and see the Spirit poured out on all flesh. This is God's desire for His body on earth. This is the destiny He has for each one of us. God has infused within us a desire to turn the world upside down for Him and to do it as His family. He wants to give the whole earth permission to find its reason for living in Him.

Burning Hearts Collide

Let's Ask Him for His Fire Together

It is one thing to comprehend this passion with our minds. It is another to know it by experience. I pray, as you read these words, that the Holy Spirit and fire would fall on you and awaken your heart to burn in a way it never has before. I pray that every ounce of mind-hindering, defiled religion would be broken right now, in the name of Jesus Christ.

If you don't know what it is to be baptized in the fire of the Holy Spirit, I pray that God's love would encounter you right now and His breath would fill your inner most being. Forgive others and receive His forgiveness. Declare the following out loud right now:

> Jesus, I give you my life. You are the One who loves me with love that is stronger than death and who defeated death for me. I give my destiny fully to You; I receive the infusion of Your holy zeal to live in a way I never have before— I want to abide with this holy fire and burning I've read about. Seal me with your radical love!
>
> I pray to be hungrier for You than anything I've ever had an appetite for in the past. I hold nothing back.

Be still, breath Him in, and allow Him to move.

3

THE CHARACTER OF JESUS

We can do prophetic acts, claim territory for Christ, yell the name of Jesus, and pray shabba *in the Holy Spirit, but we will not take the land until our character resembles His.*

Permission to Burn

There was a time when some of my zealous friends and I went on a prophetic journey for the Lord. We entered a region to plant a house of prayer and revival. We were also contending for revival on the college campuses. During one of our prayer calls, God gave a specific strategy, telling us to go and drive anointed wooden stakes into the four corners of one of the college campuses as a prophetic act. We were to do this while praying over the area and declaring the gate of the campus belonged to the Lord. As silly as this might sound, we wanted to be obedient to act on the word the Lord gave us.

Humility in Teamwork

A friend who was with us does these types of prophetic acts frequently, but he is often alone when he does them. "I do this type of thing all the time. You guys are getting in my way," he said with authority. He wanted to go about it with his normal strategy. Strife tried to enter the team. People began to argue; tears began to fall. Friends were divided and Satan was having a blast. Arguments were theological, technical, and downright immature.

We had six very fiery, burning, and passionately-in-love-with-Jesus people on this journey. Sometimes when you get that much fire together, things get heated. Feelings were hurt, and the assignment was temporarily put on hold until we could restore peace and unity among the group. While working through this issue, I spoke with my friend, who was still angry over the situation, and I told him, "We can do prophetic acts, claim territory for Christ, yell the name of Jesus, and pray *shabba* in the Holy Spirit, but we will not take the land until our character resembles His." The journey that night had more to do with learning humility and how to submit to one another and overcome

The Character of Jesus

than claiming the gates of the campus. The Lord wanted to open our eyes to the need for authentic connection, humility, and maturity.

We are temples of the Holy Spirit. We are the tools to release His power. We are the answer to the prayers Jesus prayed when He was about to be glorified: "Father, that they might be one, that the world may know it was You who sent me" (see John 17:21, paraphrased). When Jesus said He would tear down the temple and raise it up again in three days, He was speaking of His body. We, the body of Christ, are part of that temple He is raising up again. All this is so that He might manifest Himself and His love on the earth in these last days. He longs to raise up a generation of burning ones who will allow Him to manifest Himself unhindered. To be those burning ones, we must burn with the heart of Jesus.

This zeal must be sustainable as a lifestyle. The first and often repeated step is yielding to the inner cleansing of His holy fire. We must embrace the inner cleansing, not run from it. When we truly begin to hunger for God, the mess that hinders us will manifest first. This purification process often occurs before or after God releases His power through us. Don't fear the junk coming to the surface. Don't allow condemnation or accusations from the darkness to knock you down. It is the kindness of the Lord to cleanse our hearts. Simply embrace the journey of change and allow the Holy Spirit to bring forth good fruit in the time of trial. You will be amazed at how you will mature into His likeness when you stop resisting the humbling fire and embrace it instead—even when it seems like a trial from hell. Paul talked about this when he said,

> Not only that, but we rejoice in our sufferings, knowing that suffering produces endurance, and

> endurance produces character, and character produces hope, and hope does not put us to shame, because God's love has been poured into our hearts through the Holy Spirit who has been given to us.
> - Romans 5:3-5 ESV

Godly character developed through persevering in times of trial will enable us to truly take the territory for Jesus and know the glory is His alone.

Jesus's zeal for holiness is the blueprint of overcoming and accomplishing destiny by way of fiery trials.

It was the character of Christ—His purity and sinlessness—that made it possible for Him to destroy death, hell, and the grave and reclaim people for the kingdom of heaven. His complete submission to God the Father and God the Holy Spirit enabled Him to finish the work on the cross. Jesus fulfilled prophecy and performed miracles, but it was His godly character and sinless life that proved Him the Son of God.

The first-century believers performed miracles like Jesus did, but they also sought to walk in His righteousness.

> For you have been called for this purpose, since Christ also suffered for you, leaving you an example for you to follow in His steps, who committed no sin, nor was any deceit found in His mouth; and while being reviled, He did not revile in return; while suffering, He uttered no threats, but kept entrusting Himself to Him who judges righteously; and He Himself bore our sins in His body on the cross, so that we might die to sin and live to righteousness.
> - 1 Peter 2:21-24

The Character of Jesus

Since Jesus defeated death fixed on the passionate love-led vision to obey His Father and restore humankind to immortality, He remained sinless. We must also embrace trials and let them have their perfect work in us. This leads to the holy training of our minds, wills, and emotions to operate like His. This fiery process aligns our hearts and character with the holy attributes of God so that we can be without reproach.

In the Beatitudes, Jesus declared the pure in heart are blessed, for they will see God (see Matt. 5:18). I love the Beatitudes, because they give us a window into how to live in unhindered intimacy with Jesus. Pia Jo Reynolds, national mobilizer for Awaken the Dawn, described this type of intimacy this way:

> For years, I'd catch myself looking elsewhere for something I sensed was missing—something more. It was in this seemingly lonely place that I began to truly seek the voice, love, and heart of my Father. He was teaching me the importance of genuine dependency. It was there I learned that this "fire" I sensed I was missing was intended to be kindled within my own heart. This newly ignited fire did not represent a place of arrival but rather a place of new beginnings. The more I prayed, the more I spent time alone seeking His face, and the more Jesus became enough.
>
> – Pia Jo Reynolds

One essential key to persevering through trials is praying the truth of the Word of God and praying in the Spirit. Using the Word of God as our love letter and our sword will develop an inner burning that will be unquenchable. Praying in the Spirit strengthens the inner man and increases our fiery love for Him. The more we ask for His desires to be manifest in our lives, the more we will know what it is to be dissatisfied with our own stinking attitudes and behaviors, and with fleeting pleasures offered by the impure world around us. We become keenly aware that there is a true inner transformation taking place as we experience more of what it is to be insulted and falsely accused, just as Jesus was, but we also learn how to love unconditionally and forgive as He forgave. To burn for Him is to become unhindered by these things, because we know in the depths of our beings that we want Him more than we want popularity in this world. We will begin to embrace being misunderstood, because we see the beauty of character it brings and the move of God that is manifest through it all.

Know this, beloved: God is so close to the brokenhearted. The more we are broken, the more we can see Him mending us. It's like the oozing of the anointing oil from the crushed olive. As burning ones, we come to a place where we become aware of, and even truly broken over, the depravity of humankind. As we long to obey God's Word, we begin to pray for those who persecute us, and in a supernatural way, we begin to love them more and weep for them to burn for Him too. This is what it looks like to be transformed into His likeness.

Bleeding Love

I have prayed what some may consider dangerous prayers. These prayers have been for humility, wisdom, and purity of heart; and to love like He loves and hate what He hates. I have cried out to God in my pain and asked Him to make me bleed love like Jesus did when people hurt me. In my pain, I have seen a vision of Jesus stretched out on the cross, dripping love for His false accusers from His marred body. These prayers burst forth from my bleeding, burning heart in times of slander and rejection. But these moments of distress also bring me to a place of purity and humility in Him—virtues I have asked Him to develop in me. I have bled love, and I have also spewed in pain. Through it all, I have learned to run to the fire and not away from it. I have been marked by His love, and now there is no place I would rather be. If the tears take me deeper in intimacy and revelation of Him, then bring them on. Growing older in this journey, I have learned that these moments are beautiful pressings that release an oil of anointing, or empowering grace, for the life of burning I have cried out for.

This could be why I ask the Lord to fill stadiums with those who will be marked with the Spirit of burning—not just another gathering of masses of people praying cookie-cutter prayers and then falling away at the first pressing of their ego. I long to see a generation endure. I believe it is time for the outbreak of holy fire that marks people with the passion and perseverance Jesus had.

The Lord is releasing a Jesus movement that is greater than any other movement—a sustainable movement of men and women who will walk in His Spirit, wisdom, and character and burn with His passion. Signs, wonders, and miracles will happen, but these burning ones won't care to take the credit. This phenomenon will be normal to them, because they live out the Scriptures. They will simply keep seeking to know His heart in the secret place, for they know that what happens through them happens because they have been with Jesus. Likely, they will not even notice fanfare, because they will be too enamored with Jesus and His glory to care.

Permission to Burn

This type of burning does not come from attending good events or a once-a-week church service. It comes only when the burning one is hiding in the wilderness and in the caves of Psalm 91. This fire is stoked when the flaming heart longs to stay hidden, even when the spotlight is calling him or her out. This type of hunger for Jesus happens when simple converts realize their identity as sons and daughters of the Most High, and they know their worth exceeds the works they do. Lifelong burning ones feed on a lifestyle of fasting, prayer, reckless devotion to the Word, endurance in testing and trial, and most importantly, radical love for Jesus. Are we willing to live in this love that stands the test of time?

Burning like Jesus requires humility and a teachable spirit; we must learn to love reproof just as much as we love edification. If we want to be on fire and encounter God in the way He desires for us to live (and for which He died to enable us to live), then we must pursue purity, no matter the cost.

Our greatest desire has to be to set our gaze on Him and to manifest His character in and through our lives. "A good man out of the good treasure of his heart brings forth what is good; and the evil man out of the evil treasure brings forth what is evil; for his mouth speaks from that which fills his heart" (Luke 6:45). Our heart must be filled with the desire for Him to be our good treasure.

Jesus shares the treasures of living in the beauty of communion with God, now and forever. It's a great challenge to read His famous sermon slowly, yet with fervent intercession, asking God to develop each of these attitudes in our lives. Oh, that we would ask from the place of hunger for holiness and fire, knowing that the successive promises are His rewards.

The Character of Jesus

Blessed are the poor in spirit, for theirs is the kingdom of heaven.
Blessed are those who mourn, for they shall be comforted.
Blessed are the gentle, for they shall inherit the earth.
Blessed are those who hunger and thirst for righteousness, for they shall be satisfied.
Blessed are the merciful, for they shall receive mercy.
Blessed are the pure in heart, for they shall see God.
Blessed are the peacemakers, for they shall be called sons of God.
Blessed are those who have been persecuted for the sake of righteousness, for theirs is the kingdom of heaven.
Blessed are you when people insult you and persecute you, and falsely say all kinds of evil against you because of Me. Rejoice and be glad, for your reward in heaven is great; for in the same way they persecuted the prophets who were before you.
– Matthew 5:3-12

Pray

Jesus, I want to manifest Your character. Teach me to pray Your Word and create in me a longing for Your benefits. Even in my wounding, help me to bleed love. I submit to You in the time of trial and testing. I long to see Your handiwork as You forge my heart to beat in sync with Yours. Deliver me from just doing work for You. I want to ooze Your glory. May I have radical love that stands the test of time.

4

RELATIONSHIP THAT KNOWS NO BOUNDS

Tears streamed down my face, my groaning released from somewhere deep down inside my soul. Knuckles white, I gripped the altar. It was as if there was no one else in the room but the Lord. Then a wailing cry came forth. "I want nothing but you, God. Forever, you and you alone satisfy the longing of my soul! I don't need anyone but you!" I was twenty-two years old and had been apprehended by the eternal lover of my soul!

Since the creation of humanity, the Lord has been writing a love story unlike any other. It is an incredible thing to encounter the passionate agape love of God. Being touched by the manifest presence of God in this time of prayer, I felt complete. It was as if I didn't need a husband or friends, just God. But in this fiery love relationship with God, He has also made me in need of fellowship with others.

I explained this in a conversation with someone who was giving up on the prospect of marriage, the need for friends, or having a family of her own, I brought up Genesis 2:18. I asked her, "Why did God say it's not good for man to be alone if humankind had not yet sinned and had continuous and consistent fellowship with Him?"

Adam certainly was not alone; he was with God. Our most intense encounter with the Lord cannot compare to the experience of walking with God in the garden of Eden. Adam experienced constant fellowship with Him. Yet still, God said it was not good for man to be alone. Maybe, in the infinite wisdom of God, He realized people need companions in the same order of themselves, with whom they can enjoy the experience of communing with God and ruling over creation. Indeed, God knew the enjoyment His children could receive from interdependent relationships in mutual submission and dominion with the Trinity.

"The Lord God said, 'It is not good for the man to be alone; I will make him a helper suitable for him'" (Genesis 2:18). God put Adam to sleep and took a rib from his side, and from that rib, He formed the woman. When God woke Adam, he saw the woman and said, "This is now bone of my bones, and flesh of my flesh; she shall be called Woman, because she was taken out of Man" (Gen. 2:23).

Relationship That Knows No Bounds

At this moment, a divine revelation of the beauty of relationship manifested. This woman, the *ezer* or helper, was a suitable partner whom, according to the Strong's Concordance, was created to relationally come to the aid of the man; and together, they could hunger and thirst for God. Eve was created like Adam. She was made from him and given to help him govern Eden, the place of perfection. This partnership was powerful, much like the Father's partnership with the Son and the Spirit. Powerfully, we see this same Hebrew term *ezer* used for help when God refers to himself as coming to the aid of Israel (in Psalm 89:19). A simple study of the word "helper" in both the Hebrew and Greek, *parakletos*, radiates light on God as an astonishing prophetic author and master revelator. Though Adam and Eve were merely human, God was creating a storyline that ultimately directs us back to Himself, the Holy Spirit, His Son, and the end-times bride.

The Bridal Paradigm

The relationship between Adam and Eve is a compelling prophetic picture of the fellowship God designed mankind to experience with Jesus. Biblically, Jesus is referred to as the Bridegroom and His church as the bride. The ultimate romance takes place between the created son and daughter of God, as their God-given, fiery hearts burn for God and for one another. This united marriage relationship presented through Adam and Eve, and the mandate to multiply and have dominion over all creation, is also a spiritual blueprint for the fiery function of the New Testament church. He wants burning hearts to fellowship with one another and with Him in worship, prayer, learning His Word, and eating meals together. In such friendship, a bond grows between and among Him and them that is unbreakable. This is the communion between humanity and God Adam and Eve experienced, and it's God's destiny for His church. In this way, as a powerful team, Adam and Eve were designed to rule creation together. The same will be valid for us as we grasp the bridal paradigm.

When God told Adam man needed to be divided from his father and mother to be joined to his wife, He prophesied that the Bridegroom must be willing to give his life for his bride. This revelation points forward to Christ, leaving His Father in heaven and coming to die for His bride, but it also speaks to the covenant bond of human marriage. God was not only giving instruction but prophetically speaking to Adam of a time of separation that would call him to be united with his bride, who was bone of his bones and flesh of his flesh. The Father was saying, You two are one. Let no one separate you from one another. These words would soon ring true in Adam's ears when he would leave the perfect bliss of the garden, and communion with his Father, because of the spiritual death caused by sin (see Gen. 3).

I can imagine the dark and painful moment when the crisp, juicy, forbidden fruit was consumed. The serpent who is Satan laughs. Adam's eyes are opened, and he knows not only good but evil! He looks and is ashamed. He says, "What have we done? I've never felt this aching and sadness. I've never felt disappointment." Eve says, "Oh, Adam! Do you still love me? Are you angry with me? How could you have let this happen? I'm so ashamed of myself, my body, and of who I am."

Eve wails, running to hide, and Adam leaves that garden running after her. She is sewing fig leaves together in an attempt to hide her humiliation. She hands him his

Relationship That Knows No Bounds

garments and turns her head. He has become angry and begins to despise her in his heart. Suddenly, a thunderous, terrifying sound fills the area. Loving yet terrifying conviction falls. Father says, "Where are you, Adam?" Adam remembers the words God spoke to him: "For this reason a man shall leave his father and his mother, and be joined to his wife; and they shall become one flesh" (Gen. 2:24). Now the Father would come to them but with a much more difficult covenant. The challenge to cleave to one another would now be a struggle. God was bringing a divine, prophetic revelation and warning to His son, Adam, that he was alone and incomplete without his wife.

This relationship surpasses any other in creation. The uniting of a man and woman in marriage is a prophetic theme that runs throughout the Old and New Testaments. The bride is an image of the church, and the bridegroom is an image of Jesus the Son, the second Adam. The story of separation and reunion climaxed at the cross of Calvary. The sinless Bridegroom took on the sin of the world to be reunited with His bride. I call it the bridal paradigm. This is the dramatic course of action the Father and Son took to restore unity with humanity, which was broken by sin and temptation in the garden. (I will discuss the bridal paradigm more in the next chapter.)

United, passionate fellowship of the brethren with the Messiah is a revelatory visual of the bride and the Bridegroom ruling together. This was revealed to Peter.

> When Jesus came into the district of Caesarea Philippi, He was asking His disciples, "Who do people say that the Son of Man is?" And they said, "Some say John the Baptist; and others, Elijah; but still others, Jeremiah, or one of the prophets." He said to them, "But who do you say that I am?"

> Simon Peter answered, "You are the Christ, the Son of the living God."
>
> And Jesus said to him, "Blessed are you, Simon Barjona, because flesh and blood did not reveal this to you, but My Father who is in heaven. I also say to you that you are Peter, and upon this rock I will build My church; and the gates of Hades will not overpower it. I will give you the keys of the kingdom of heaven; and whatever you bind on earth shall have been bound in heaven, and whatever you loose on earth shall have been loosed in heaven." Then He warned the disciples that they should tell no one that He was the Christ.
>
> - Matthew 16:13-20

Peter heard from heaven that Jesus is not just a man or another prophet, but He is the awaited Son of God and the Messiah. In response, Jesus told Peter (my paraphrase of vv. 17-20): This revelation was from My Father in heaven; it was not of flesh and blood. This heavenly revelation will transform you and everyone who hears it. Your identity will never be the same, because you have heard from My Father. I will call you Petros, for it is on this rock of divine revelation that I will build My church, or ekklesia. When My church hears from the Father like you have, Peter, then I will rebuild and establish my dominion through her in the earth, just like I did with Adam and Eve. When this happens, the gates of hell will not prevail against it.

Jesus referred to Simon as Peter, which means "a piece of the rock" or one of the "living stones" that would build up the spiritual house of His presence. His spiritual house is not a building, His house is His people—sons and

Relationship That Knows No Bounds

daughters who will arise to be the holy priesthood containing the very presence of God on the earth. Peter later wrote about this.

> As you come to him, the living Stone—rejected by humans, but chosen by God and precious to him—you also, like living stones, are being built into a spiritual house to be a holy priesthood, offering spiritual sacrifices acceptable to God through Jesus Christ. For in Scripture it says: "See, I lay a stone in Zion, a chosen and precious cornerstone, and the one who trusts in him will never be put to shame."
>
> – 1 Peter 2:4-6 NIV

Jesus went on to exhort Peter concerning this pivotal revelation, saying that Peter and all who believe in Christ will build His *ekklesia,* and the gates of hell will not prevail against it. He was not referring to another physical building but to a people who would burn for Him in a place of constant revelation of Him. Jesus acknowledged the revelation from heaven Peter received because this is the miracle that will call men and women of God and cause them to walk in true unity with one another. The key is in not only knowing the Messiah individually but also hearing from heaven together, seeking the face of God in one accord. Jesus was saying, in a sense, that when we live in a place of heavenly revelation of Him *together,* even the most unimaginable evil cannot stop the advancement of His kingdom or His people.

The power of this passage is the revelation of who Jesus is, which came from the Father in heaven to a mortal human. In this revelation, the keys of the kingdom were given to bind and loose and to restore dominion to God's people (see Matthew 18:18). Jesus was talking to Peter in

Permission to Burn

Matthew 16 about more than just figuring out who He is or what people say about Him. Jesus was promising that those who continually meet in a place of revelation and with burning hearts will not be shaken by what people think or say about them or about Jesus. He exhorted Peter and the apostles to be passionate together and to be the living stones He can build upon. That place of holy community is where Christ can do His will among His people. Jesus pointed to Peter and then towards—the worst of the worst in Caesarea, Philippi—and said that if they would receive this revelation from heaven and do it, even hell would not prevail against them.

In this way, Jesus was awakening His disciples on the inside, opening their spiritual eyes to the same revelation God awakened inside Adam.

It is not good for people to be alone. Jesus stood among them as the source of salvation—One who would restore them to burning-heart fellowship with Him and one another, as He does today. Ultimately, as we read in the book of Revelation, Jesus will return for His bride, His promised one.

In the meantime, our mission is communion with Him and with one another and, from that place, expansion of the kingdom of God on earth. We can and must be able to hunger and thirst for our relationship with God alone. We should burn with fiery passion for Him, even if we are exiled, as John the Beloved was when he penned the book of Revelation. But we must not neglect the powerful and complete dynamic of pursuing Him with others. I believe this is why Jesus included loving others in His statement about the greatest commandment. He said, "You shall love the Lord your God with all your heart, and with all your soul, and with all your mind, and with all your strength . . .

Relationship That Knows No Bounds

[and] you shall love your neighbor as yourself" (Mark 12:30-31).

In Ecclesiastes, we find another statement that it is not good for people to be alone:

> Two are better than one because they have a good return for their labor. For if either of them falls, the one will lift up his companion. But woe to the one who falls when there is not another to lift him up. Furthermore, if two lie down together they keep warm, but how can one be warm alone? And if one can overpower him who is alone, two can resist him. A cord of three strands is not quickly torn apart.
>
> – Ecclesiastes 4:9-12

This is the fellowship of the burning heart. It looks like keeping one another warm and stoking the fire in each other's hearts. Just as the Father, Son, and Holy Spirit are three in one, so are we with Him as the family of God. Tightly wrapped around Him, we—the *ekklesia*, the bride, the church—are the three-stranded cord that is not easily broken. We are the force the gates of hell cannot prevail against. This is bigger than marriage. The biblical marriage and family picture is a prophetic anaolgy of unity within the bride of Christ. As we unite with one another and hunger for Him and for His righteousness and His will to be done, and as we bear a pure and holy passion for Jesus's dominion on the earth, Satan is brought to terror.

What we must understand is that we cannot hope to love one another or love Him without His Spirit in us. Carnal unity alone does not cut it; just ask the people who built the Tower of Babel! Anyone can unite around a common theme, but only the vision of heaven will prevail.

Permission to Burn

After I was raped, people united to silence me, destroy me, and cover up the evil, but the revelation of Jesus in my life has silenced and scattered my accusers. The Lord will destroy false unity movements.

We must know that world-changing unity does not compromise the message of Christ. True oneness is accomplished, as Zechariah prophesied to Zerubbabel, "'not by might nor by power, but by My spirit,' (Zech. 4:6). We must know that "unless the Lord builds the house, they labor in vain who build it" (Ps. 127:1).

Submit One to Another

In an old, dusty barroom, we gathered. The brick floors and the old bar remained. I could almost smell cigarette smoke and alcohol. Sounds of loud music and cries for Jesus broke me out of the past, and I laughed at the irony. This was the place where I once was lost and inebriated. Now I was hosting an all-night worship and prayer event. The presence of God was so thick. We crammed into the small space for one thing—to glorify Jesus. The old bar had shut down and been turned into a church. The church welcomed us to host the presence of God and gave us no time limits.

Over the past few years, God has given me the privilege of traveling and holding twenty-four-hour continuous worship and prayer events with ministry leaders, worshipers, prayer warriors, musicians, and singers from different ministries and backgrounds. He's given me the opportunity to gather together those who love Him for twenty-four hours of fellowship in His presence. Through these meetings, we have received such powerful revelations of His desire to obliterate hindrances like denominations, theologies, and religious formulas. During these meetings,

Relationship That Knows No Bounds

the hearts of the people have been knit together so strongly by the power of being in His presence that we use the word *family* when we talk about it with one another. Just twenty-four hours of being with our Father together, with no agenda, causes the walls of division to come tumbling down.

We cannot build this *ekklesia*/church-burning community for our own benefit. We must build it together by God's Spirit through His revelation from heaven. He gives His blueprint to His people, the church, whom the gates of hell cannot prevail against.

First, we must understand that divine restoration and unity will not happen unless we are in constant fellowship with His Spirit. This gives us permission to burn unhindered like we never have before. But we must choose to burn in submission one to another with the Spirit of God. We must allow Him to be the head of this movement, His church, and we must come into alignment with Him, His heavenly vision, and one another. "The Spirit and the bride say, 'Come!' And let the one who hears say, "Come!" Let the one who is thirsty come; and let the one who wishes take the free gift of the water of life . . . He who testifies to these things says, 'Yes, I am coming soon.' Amen. Come, Lord Jesus" (Revelation 22:17,20).

This is the story of the Bridegroom calling to His bride through His Spirit who lives inside her. He is calling her to return to Him in unity with one another, without spot or blemish, because it is His desire to come to her. His bride is the body of believers who are in fellowship and burning with one another, with His Spirit in their hearts, crying together for a reunited manifestation in the flesh of what has been broken.

God is calling us to a fellowship of the burning hearts. It is beautiful when we can burn for Him and with one another, not fearing what people will say or do. The Scriptures say, "Can two walk together, unless they are agreed?" (Amos 3:3 NKJV). I believe we are in a moment in time when God is bringing the church into agreement through the prayer movement (day-and-night prayer and worship) and bringing us into the place of fellowship with one another in His presence. In His presence, we find freedom. All division will disappear when brothers and sisters in Christ remove the weights (sins) that hinder them. When these sins are no longer an issue, we will be able to focus fully on His face. We will be able to simply worship Him. We must lay aside our agendas and ask Him for His. It's time for us to come into agreement with one another and burn together. It's time for an awakening in our hearts so we can know how to be in unity with the brethren, which results from being in unity with heaven.

Where there is a misunderstanding, the Lord brings understanding, forgiveness, and reconciliation by the power of His Spirit. This revelation is awakening in the hearts of His people, enabling them to lay down their differences and enter into a place of worship and prayer that brings unity. This unity has absolutely nothing to do with merely tolerating one another. Oneness is allowing the presence of God to awaken our hearts to love one another, in a fresh experience. In His presence, repentance and reconciliation become more real than the air we breathe. This is not fake tolerance or lukewarm political handshaking that appears to be unity but is not. This is real!

In His presence, we find fullness of joy and unconditional love. In His presence, we can reestablish the

Relationship That Knows No Bounds

foundation King David set into place when he established a tent of meeting for the nation to encounter the presence of God (see 1 Chron. 15:1-29). King David established day-and-night prayer and worship as the foundation of a place of meeting. In God's presence, we find freedom, deliverance, and true awakening (see 2 Cor. 3:17).

When we allow God to move however He desires, competition ceases. This is why we must learn to minister to God before we minister to people. Corporate worship and prayer, infused with His Word and guided by His Spirit, build a movement that hell can't stop. In this place, we find the freedom to burn together for Him. Making prayer and worship the foundation allows us to love each other with the love of God in a way that cannot be accomplished by mere human wisdom or mental understanding of the Scriptures. This is why He gave us His Spirit—to awaken us to His heart. He moves "not by might nor by power, but by my Spirit" (Zech. 4:6 NIV).

It's amazing to me that God is three persons in one, interdependent within Himself, yet dependent on no one. He chooses to work together with Himself but in the form of the three persons of the Trinity. I wonder if God chose this dynamic to teach us what it is to truly love. The Father gives Himself to work together with the Word (the Son) and the Spirit (His own life-giving breath) to build something above and beyond amazing.

God loves pure submission and authentic unity. When He created Adam, He said, "It is not good for the man to be alone" (Gen. 2:18). In the creation of man, He made a statement that would become a thread woven throughout eternity. Even in eternity, God the Trinity paints a picture of the three-in-one. He is the master artist and storyteller, and His stories are always bigger than we think. His stories are trustworthy and true and divinely prophetic. Even the statement that it is not good for man to be alone speaks volumes. He is such a humble God. In all His wonder, He reevaluates His creation, the one made in His image, and says "I can do better than this."

This is the story of a true family that lacks nothing when synchronized in beautiful heart-to-heart submission—the Son submitting to the Father, the Spirit submitting to the Son, and the Son laying down His life for His bride. Therefore, the bride may be full of God's Spirit to be united in full submission to one another and to rule the earth together, passionately in love, forever. Part of the beauty of burning is in not burning alone; it is the exhilaration found in the fellowship of burning hearts.

It is not suitable for man to be alone; we need one another.

Pray

> I repent, Lord, of any wounds that may keep me from enjoying the bliss of a fiery community. Deliver me of jealousy, judgment, and cynicism. Ignite my heart with a passionate love for You, and allow me to see Your heart for Your bride. Soften my heart if it has been hardened. Holy Spirit, have Your way in my heart. I don't want false unity. I don't want to just tolerate people. I want to love as passionately as You do.

Take a few moments to listen to the still, small voice of the Lord. You may have a painful moment come to mind. Possibly, you hear a name or place. God may be healing a marriage or family relationship.

Relationship That Knows No Bounds

Pray This

> Jesus, I forgive _____. I am not _____'s judge, you are. Forgive me for holding the offense against _____. That offense has kept me from forming authentic relationships. I place the cross between myself and _____. Make my heart tender again. Restore my broken relationships to help me to trust again. Lord, I cry out to you to bring me together with others in a burning, godly community. Help me experience the beauty of the bridal fellowship.

5
Love-Sick Warriors

The backseat of their car is so confining. All the ladies laugh with excitement, but I want out. Trying to hide my sadness, I look at my phone again. I whisper, "There is no signal in the high mountains?" The vehicle stops. I hike down the gravel road, dialing his number again and again. He answers, but he can't hear my voice. I want to go home.

Permission to Burn

Have you ever been so in love that it made your heart sick to be separated from the one who had your heart? When I first married my husband, I went away on a retreat for a couple of days. Even though it was a short time apart, I literally ached on the inside and wept in the night, yearning to be with him.

The truth is that when we fall in love, our hearts are so firmly knit together with another human that being separated from that person doesn't feel natural. Yearning for our lover presents an experience of urgency. God put that aching in us to remind us that it is not good to be alone. He pens within us a prophetic gripping for love that can ultimately be filled by Him alone. The bond within marriage is a picture of intimacy that we are designed to have eternally with God.

The Torment of Separation

The aching of our hearts for one another, and the depths of love and even pain we feel in separation, are physical examples of the spiritual connection in our relationship with our heavenly Father. His love for us is so deep that He went to the most extreme measure to be reunited with us. He was tormented by our separation from Him, which was caused by our sin. He wasn't tormented because He needed us. He is completely whole in Himself. The aching of His heart is because He loves us and wants us. He wants us! He chooses us! There is so much freedom. He allowed Himself to feel the grief of His separation from us, and He acted because of it. When Jesus came and died, He chose to experience torment so that He would not need to remain separated from us.

When I began to grasp the power of the revelation of the true gospel message, which started in Genesis and

LOVE-SICK WARRIORS

carried through to Revelation, I saw the depth of love God had for Adam and Eve in the way He responded to their disobedience and sin in the garden. In Genesis 3, we see that even in their temptation and resulting disobedience, God never turned His back on His son and daughter. Instead, He came after them, calling out to them. They were hiding from Him. He never rejected them or pulled away from them. *He came to them.*

He even shed the blood of an animal to cover their sin. This was the second time blood was shed. The first happened when God put Adam into a deep sleep and created Eve—that was the first pure covenant relationship, resulting in life and family. The second time of bloodshed was a time of agony. God sacrificed His own creation so He could use the skins of animals to cover their sin. Covenant and consecration are costly, even to God.

I believe it saddened the heart of God to have to shed the blood of His precious, innocent animals, but He wanted to cover the nakedness and shame of His son and daughter. Now, not only did they know good, but they had also been awakened to the existence of evil. They were supposed to have dominion and rule the earth, not let it rule them. But I believe the torment of separation played a big part in the redemptive covenant God made with His disobedient children. They were no longer able to live forever, at least not without God sacrificing Himself for them. He did this later when He stepped out of heaven and put on the flesh of mankind to give His life in the form of the incarnation of Jesus Christ.

The amazing thing about the sovereignty of God is that this situation did not take Him by surprise. In fact, the Word says the Lamb, the perfect sacrifice, in Jesus Christ, was slain before the foundation of the earth (see Rev. 13:8).

Permission to Burn

That's the amazing thing about our Father: He has always had a plan for how to deal with our disobedience.

I believe the most heartbreaking thing to our Father is to be separated from His beloved sons and daughters. He never chooses separation from us. In our shame and sin, we choose separation from Him. As Paul said, "For the wages of sin is death, but the free gift of God is eternal life in Christ Jesus our Lord" (Rom. 6:23).

The Bridal Longing

Solomon wildly expressed the torment of separation and the provoking longing between the bride and the Bridegroom.

> [Bridegroom:] I have come into my garden, my sister, my bride; I have gathered my myrrh along with my balsam. I have eaten my honeycomb and my honey; I have drunk my wine and my milk. Eat, friends; drink and imbibe deeply, O lovers.
>
> [Bride:] I was asleep but my heart was awake. A voice! My beloved was knocking: "Open to me, my sister, my darling, my dove, my perfect one! For my head is drenched with dew, my locks with the damp of the night." I have taken off my dress, how can I put it on again? I have washed my feet; how can I dirty them again? My beloved extended his hand through the opening, and my feelings were aroused for him. I arose to open to my beloved; and my hands dripped with myrrh, and my fingers with liquid myrrh, on the handles of the bolt. I opened to my beloved, but my beloved had turned away and had gone! My heart went out to him as he spoke. I searched for him but I did not find him; I

called him but he did not answer me. The watchmen who make the rounds in the city found me, they struck me and wounded me; the guardsmen of the walls took away my shawl from me. I adjure you, O daughters of Jerusalem, if you find my beloved, as to what you will tell him: For I am lovesick.

[Daughters of Jerusalem:] What kind of beloved is your beloved, O most beautiful among women? What kind of beloved is your beloved, that thus you adjure us?
– Song of Solomon 5:1-9

In this passage, we experience the bride and the bridegroom being captivated by the torment of being separated from one another. The entire book of the Song of Solomon is a picture of Jesus the Bridegroom pursuing the church, His bride. This book is the most powerful prophetic romance book in the Bible. It almost seems explicit at times, but the Lord divinely inspired Solomon to write this to prove His desperation to be with His bride. Some Bible versions call this book the Song of all Songs. It truly is the greatest song—a love song to woo His people, His bride, and awaken her to His relentless love for her. In my Bible, this portion of Scripture is appropriately titled "The Torment of Separation."

Over and over, Solomon spoke of this love that shouldn't be awakened until the beloved (the bride) is ready, because once awakened, this jealous love cannot be put out. It is jealous, and it fights to be the only love. Even death is not stronger than this love. It is the kind of love that makes her willing to be beaten in order to be reunited with the one she loves. It is not a weak and mushy, selfish love; it is a strong, fiery, jealous love. It is a passionate love and a warrior's love. Only a warrior's love would cause a man to lay down his life.

Such love provokes those who do not know God to jealousy and anger. This is the love of God, the love He awakens in His church—the love of the bride for His Son. In Song of Solomon, the bride goes out searching for her love at night, and she is beaten for being out in the streets at night. She tells the daughters of Jerusalem, "If you find my beloved, as to what you will tell him: for I am lovesick."

In context, this passage is often interpreted as being about God's chosen one, Israel, being provoked to jealousy by the Gentiles, who have found love like no other in the Messiah.

> I say then, they did not stumble so as to fall, did they? May it never be! But by their transgression salvation has come to the Gentiles, to make them jealous. Now if their transgression is riches for the world and their failure is riches for the Gentiles, how much more will their fulfillment be! But I am speaking to you who are Gentiles. Inasmuch then as I am an apostle of Gentiles, I magnify my ministry, if somehow I might move to jealousy my fellow countrymen and save some of them. For if their rejection is the reconciliation of the world, what will their acceptance be but life from the dead?
>
> – Romans 11:11-15

This love is supposed to provoke them to jealousy so they can see and know He has come. Oh, the glory and blessing that will be poured out upon the earth as their jealousy arouses them to accept Jesus as their awaited

Love-Sick Warriors

Messiah! Beloved, even in persecution, we search in the night and call for His return. Our response to suffering should be, "Oh, Jerusalem, if you see Him, tell Him I am love-sick! I will search all through the night, until I find the one I love, and when I find Him, I won't let him go!"

This is the passion I have been talking about. We have permission from the Lord to give our lives for this zeal. I cry out for an awakening of this in each of our hearts, that we may have the same love for Him that He has for us. Once it is awakened, this love will cause us to give our lives and never let go. Many don't understand the radical, laid-down, lover lifestyle, because it has not yet been awakened in their hearts. But Jesus is singing to each one of us, "You have stolen my heart, my sister my bride; you have stolen my heart with one glance of your eyes" (Song 4:9 NIV). He's captivated by us, and He longs for us to be captivated by Him.

I declare: Awaken love now, in Jesus's name! You have permission to burn. The Spirit of the Lord says, *Permission to burn, My bride! Yes! Burn radically for Me! Seek Me and you will find Me. Knock and the door will be opened when you search with all your heart* (see Matt. 7:7).

The love story began in the garden of Eden, but it didn't stop there. Adam and Eve were a prophetic picture of the bride and the Bridegroom. When God put the man to sleep and pierced his side to extract his bride, He was creating a prophetic masterpiece with this love story that would climax on the cross. This love story continued in a garden with an empty tomb and the powerful resurrected appearance of the Bridegroom, Jesus, to the weeping, love-sick Mary. Finally, the prophetic romance made its eternal declaration in Revelation, when the Bridegroom said, "Yes, I am coming quickly" (Rev. 22:20). When the second

Adam, Jesus, the Son of God, successfully fulfilled the mission to pursue His bride through the darkness of sin, to reverse the curse, He remained sinless, unlike Adam. He gave His life to redeem her. He left His Father to go and take back His bride.

Close your eyes and look at the cross of Calvary. See your Bridegroom, Jesus, hanging lifelessly. Now see the soldiers walking up to His body and piercing His side to confirm He is in the deep sleep of death. Do you see it? The prophecy is fulfilled: "'It is not good for man to be alone. I will make a helper suitable for him,' and he put Adam into a deep sleep and took from his side a rib" (Gen. 2:18, 21, my paraphrase). In the Messiah's deep sleep of death on the cross, God pierced His side to give Him back His bride.

Also, in the moments before His death, the veil in the temple built by human hands, where God's presence dwelled, was torn from top to bottom. This veil separating the bride from Christ was destroyed in the instant He breathed His last breath. Now, hear His voice crying out just moments before His death, "My God, my God, why have you forsaken Me?" Here, Jesus realized the torment of separation the sin of the world causes (see Matt. 27:46). His Father turned His head because He could not look on sin. But now, hear Him saying with relief, "It is finished! Unto you I commit my Spirit," knowing it was all worth it (see Luke 23:46; John 19:30). The pain of separation from His Father was worth the victory—that He might bridge the great divide and be joined with His bride.

The Scriptures say the earth quaked and grew dark at that moment, which was actually the day of Passover. At that very time, the priest would have been slaying a Passover lamb; meanwhile, the one true Lamb of God was being slain for the sins of the entire world. The perfect sacrifice had been made. This was the only way humanity could be unified with God again for all of eternity. Jesus's death tore down the physical temple of His body, yet in three days He would rise again. When He did, it was as a temple that would soon be united with His bride. Thankfully, it did not end here. This was just a new beginning.

In the torment of separation, He defeated death. "O death, where is your victory? O death, where is your sting?" (1 Cor. 15:55). The curse of sin and death are broken. Now we can go back into the garden with Him. We are now His temple, a temple not built with human hands, but one of His own flesh and bone, purchased by His own blood. As His temple, we are now free from the torment of separation from Him. (Really, that is what hell ultimately is—a place of torment because of separation from Him.) By the power of the Holy Spirit, we can be gripped with the revelation of what actually happened on the cross. When we do, we will be enamored!

THE BIGGEST TRAGEDY

In the beginning of this book, I wrote about the infilling of the Holy Spirit and the dramatic change the apostle Peter experienced after Jesus breathed on him and said, "Receive the Holy Spirit" (John 20:22). The infilling, or baptism, of the Holy Spirit and fire began the most powerful revival that would ever sweep the earth. This breath of God ushered in the boldness of redemption to the earth. Orphanhood could cease to exist, because people could now be adopted as sons and daughters of God. First, Jesus removed sin through His blood. Second, through His resurrection and ascension, Jesus released the promise of

His Spirit and poured it out on and into His people. In Acts 2, we see it—the greatest revival, the biggest mass harvest to sweep a region.

One of the biggest tragedies of the church today is the teaching that the gifts have ceased and that the Holy Spirit operates only for conviction of sin. The Holy Spirit is the very breath of God that brings life into these broken, fallible bodies. It is His Spirit that makes us living temples of His glory and witnesses to His mighty works in the earth, for generations. The Scriptures say, "Do you not know that you are a temple of God and that the Spirit of God dwells in you?" (1 Cor. 3:16). Furthermore, Paul wrote of "Christ in you, the hope of glory" (Col. 1:27). In the Old Testament, Habakkuk prophesied, "For the earth will be filled with the knowledge of the glory of the Lord, as the waters cover the sea" (Hab. 2:14). This can only happen as we become the hope of glory by being witnesses to Christ's power and loving one another by His Spirit. This is how the gospel is preached in a real, tangible way. It is a tragic, false doctrine that has explained away the breath of God and His function.

The believers were gathered together in obedience to Jesus in the place of prayer, waiting on the promise of the Father to come—His Spirit (Acts 1). By that time, Jesus had already breathed on the disciples, but now they were in the place of prayer for ten days, waiting in prayer and in unity. This could not have happened without the power of His Spirit working in and through them. These are the same men who ran scared when Jesus was being nailed to the cross. *Something major had changed.* They had become true inward witnesses of Jesus the Messiah, and they had been wrecked by His Spirit. They were more alive than they'd ever been—because of the Holy Spirit living within them.

LOVE-SICK WARRIORS

We can't arbitrarily pick which parts of Jesus's words we want to believe. That's heresy! It's *all* truth. And the truth is, the Holy Spirit is still alive and active in believers today. Jesus told His disciples, "You will receive power when the Holy Spirit has come upon you; and you shall be My witnesses both in Jerusalem, and in all Judea and Samaria, and even to the remotest part of the earth" (Acts 1:8). All Christians believe in preaching the gospel, but here Jesus added that we would also be His witnesses. This is impossible without His Spirit. That is what Jesus meant when He said it was better for Him to go away, so that the Helper (the Spirit) could come and enable us to be witnesses (see John 16:7).

The men, women, and children interceding in the upper room had encountered life—the *ruach hakodesh*, or Holy Spirit, who was present at the dawn of creation. Because of this, they persevered in prayer, believing for the outpouring prophesied in Joel 2. On the day of Pentecost, which was the celebration of Moses giving the law, the outpouring finally happened. In this way, the feast of Pentecost was fulfilled by the outpouring of the Holy Spirit, which brings freedom from the law by fulfilling it, and gives us grace (empowerment) for righteous living.

The outpouring of the Spirit surpassed what the law written on tablets could do. From that day forward, the law, or the Word, would be written on the hearts of God's people. Now, humanity can be full of the Spirit of God, which causes their desire for righteousness to spring from love-sickness for God, not from legalism and fear. This is a glorious freedom but also a great responsibility with great accountability.

When Jesus poured out His Spirit, people began to speak in tongues as if they were drunk. They were inebriated with the joyful, pure wine of the Holy One. It must have been an amazing time of joy and burning together in true community (communion in unity). Suddenly, they were preaching the gospel in every language. It probably felt like chaos, but to God it was a beautifully synchronized sound of revival. Thousands were saved at a time when it was dangerous to know Jesus. Many of these people would later give their lives for the cause of Christ, not because of what they knew in their heads, but because of the power and love they witnessed from the inside out.

These believers burned with holy love and fire, a gift given to them to prove their identity as sons and daughters (no longer orphans). They were alive in a way they had never been before, and they had discovered something greater than the temporary life of striving to be accepted according to the law. They were born again, not just of water but of the Spirit. Now, everything in them craved to be pure in heart so they might see God. Their hearts were on fire. In that moment of salvation, I imagine all the sermons and words Jesus had spoken to them began to flood their minds and hearts with divine revelation. They began to *get it* in the same way Peter did on that day at Caesarea, Philippi. I can hear their voices shouting with joy and weeping, "You were and still are the Christ, the Son of the living God!" They had hope of something greater.

6
Holy Dissatisfaction

Those with burning hearts refuse to be satisfied with anything less than the manifest presence of God. True burning ones are marked with an insatiable hunger for the one, true, holy God. That hunger stretches beyond the need for personal comfort, gain, fame, or preaching platforms. Often, these ones have a growing desire to stay hidden in their prayer closets, where intimacy with the Lord abounds daily. These burning ones have inscribed within their DNA a groaning for generations beyond them to be born again into the glorious promised land contained in the "on earth as it is in heaven" reality that Jesus promised. – see Matt. 6:10

Permission to Burn

The more I grew as a believer, the hungrier I became to build relationships with people who were also experiencing this ravenous hunger for the presence of God. At one time, I wanted friends who would hang out and party with me. Now I wanted friends who would call heaven to earth with me. I longed for a family of burning hearts. As I spent more time in prayer and in the study of God's Word, I became dissatisfied with the compromised reality of God's people. My worldview had been ruined in a holy way by encounters with the truth. The Word of God and the truth were no longer words in a book. The Word—the way, the truth, and the life—was the person of Jesus burning in my innermost being, and He possessed my life. I was love-sick and wrecked by the reality that He really meant every word and promise He had spoken. Childlike faith began to explode in me, and at the same time, my prophetic spiritual eyes began to open, and my walk with Him began to mature. God began progressively opening my eyes to the errors His people were walking in—much like what happened when Josiah read the Word of God for the first time and realized Israel was up to its ears in idolatry (see 2 Kings 22). I could hardly handle all the unholy compromise I saw.

My "normal" involved consuming the Word and living the lifestyle of prayer and fasting. Though I felt frustrated, I knew my dissatisfaction was somehow holy. God had pierced my heart with a desire that reached far beyond my own life—a desire for every person on the earth to know all that is available to the sons and daughters of God. For me, it wasn't about signs, wonders, and miracles, although they followed as the Scriptures said they would. This burning in my innermost being was about relationship, intimacy, and spiritual inheritance.

Holy Dissatisfaction

This inheritance is not one of land and possessions but of unbroken day-and-night fellowship with the lover of our souls. I believed everything I read in the Bible as absolute truth, and I was ruined with the desire for the whole earth to be awakened to the passionate Bridegroom, Jesus. Like Isaiah, I could not keep silent before the Lord. "For Zion's sake I will not keep silent, and for Jerusalem's sake I will not keep quiet, until her righteousness goes forth like brightness, and her salvation like a torch that is burning. The nations will see your righteousness, and all kings your glory" (Isaiah 62:1-2). "On your walls, O Jerusalem, I have appointed watchmen; all day and all night they will never keep silent. You who remind the Lord, take no rest for yourselves; and give Him no rest until He establishes and makes Jerusalem a praise in the earth" (Isaiah 62:6-7).

Day and night, I would not give Him rest until He manifested Himself in the earth and His people saw Him in all His glory. I became a flame of unquenchable fire. Little did I know I was marked with His bridal message and His longing for the spiritual birthing of His global burning family.

The Value in Movements of Old

The restoration of the broken family of God is very important; it must take place in our generation. In past movements, great strides were made to restore the family of God and the lost and to remind them of important revelation and teaching in the Scriptures. True God encounters and visitations, much like the ones I have experienced, marked the movements of old too.

God is a merciful and amazing Father who sovereignly awakens hunger in the hearts of His people, generation after generation. Because of His goodness, I believe He often moves upon the hearts of young messengers to arise, to answer the prayers of their ancestors. The prayers of the saints of old are holy incense, still rising to His nostrils. The ones we deem mighty in the Lord today could quite possibly be the manifestation of the answered travailing prayers of great-grandmas and great-grandpas in the faith who cried out for the next generation. God blesses those He chooses with a gut-wrenching, holy dissatisfaction. This holy dissatisfaction grips the heart and life, and the vessel of His glory refuses to be comforted by anything less than the truth of His Word and the reality of His fiery, glorious inner workings in humanity.

Movements have been birthed by holy, dissatisfied prayer warriors. The Reformation trumpeted the message that salvation is given through grace by faith in Jesus Christ. Martin Luther, who was ruined with desire to see the truth prevail, nailed his Ninety-Five Theses on the door of the Catholic Church. He refused to be comforted by what he viewed as a false theological existence in his generation.

Revivalists such as John Wesley, Johnathan Edwards, and George Whitfield were leaders in the First Great Awakening between 1730 and 1740. This awakening emphasized repentance and heartfelt devotion to God, as well as the necessity of the fear of God and the fire of God. The outpouring of the Holy Spirit and the breaking down of racial, gender, and denominational barriers also marked this awakening.

The waning of the First Awakening caused the desperation and hunger in people that birthed the Second Great Awakening around 1790. Many believe this began in secret in homes and prayer closets, as African Americans and women joined together, fervently praying for the

Holy Dissatisfaction

outpouring of the Holy Spirit and fire (Matthew 3:11). Holiness was trumpeted from the rooftops, and because of this awakening, the civil war eventually erupted and slaves gained their freedom. Some African Americans were recognized as spiritual leaders, and women began to have the freedom to pray, preach, and vote. Many bars and brothels shut down. Another generation was marked with hunger for God. Even as the awakening subsided, some people refused to be satisfied.

After that, the Word of Faith movement came forth, putting an important emphasis on divine healing. Oral Roberts, Katherine Kuhlman, and others in the charismatic movement restored emphasis to the gifts of the Spirit. Next, the Shepherding Movement emerged, reminding the church of the need for pastoral leaders and spiritual fathers and mothers. Currently, the prayer movement is restoring the foundation of day-and-night prayer and worship, and the apostolic and prophetic movement is awakening the body to the fullness of the fivefold ministry gifts. These are all very important.

It is important to acknowledge that after the initial pioneers of these movements passed the torch, weaknesses and abuses sometimes arose. In one way or another, all moves of God are flawed by human vessels, because after all, we are human. This doesn't take God by surprise. He chooses to work through broken human vessels. God doesn't stop moving when revivals seem to fizzle. He's always drawing the hearts of His people, generation after generation.

Considering this, we can't be so arrogant as to believe we will not mess up this current move God is birthing through us. Sadly, in many instances today, we find ourselves trying to undo false teachings that have crept into the church because of arrogance, but we forget the possibility that we, too, may fall into the same fleshly trap. At times, teachings contain more deception than truth, because pride creeps into our hearts. Many fall prey to the temptation to use the move of God for personal benefit. In the words of Paul to the church of Galatia, we become foolish and forget we began this good work by the grace of God in the Spirit, and as a result, we find ourselves trying to be "perfected by the flesh" (Gal. 3:3). The human desire to build one's own kingdom slithers into the teachings, and before we know it, a Tower of Babel is being built.

This causes the next generation to grow up in confusion because of distorted and divisive language. Ultimately, the next generation then develops its own language in hopes of gaining an identity. Because of this, teachings arise to swing the pendulum back in the other direction, resulting in a time of seeming rebellion. However, the hidden burning ones remain—a remnant that sees and hears with spiritual eyes. They cry out in their hiddenness, and fire burns in their bones to see God arise again. They see the swinging from one extreme to another, which creates a cycle of confusion and division, and they pray for God's true unity and humility to come to His church.

Each generation must claim its own holy fire. Its people must discover the Word of God and understand how it applies to them and their God-given purpose. In this process, God desires that every generation would honor the last and learn from its mistakes, never disregarding the pure foundation work in the pioneering. In other words, as the adage goes, don't throw the baby out with the bathwater. All is not bad! Purity of any confusing language is essential, but if it's biblical, we must not do away with it. We must learn how to receive a heavenly language and be

Holy Dissatisfaction

in unity with God, letting Him show us how to build upon the righteous works of the past and letting Him remove the unrighteousness. We must know that all true revelation from heaven is founded in study of the Scriptures and conceived within the messenger through fervent prayer mingled with tears.

Passing the Torch

After years of itinerate ministry and hosting twenty-four-hour nonstop prayer, worship, and revival gatherings all over the southeast, my husband and I launched a ministry base. The public launching event exploded with a powerful declaration witnessed by a multigenerational, multicultural, and multidenominational group of people. Following the heart of the Lord, we gathered for twenty-four hours of worship, prayer, and declaration of the Word. In the first two hours, the Lord trumpeted this message: "Now is the time, and this is the hour. I give you permission to burn!"

The microphone passed seamlessly between different ministers and worship leaders who sang, taught, declared, preached, and prayed. Young people flooded the altar, crying out to God in a prayer of thanksgiving that they were released to burn for Him, unhindered. Then those from the older generation came to stand behind these young ones when a prophetic invitation was released for those who would mentor, but not limit, the young people's deep longing to burn for Jesus. It was as if a message arose from the voice of the Father for these young, burning pioneers, and the old limitations of being placed in religious boxes were broken.

However, this declaration was not limited to the youth or college students. It rang out clear into the hearts of people of every age, gender, and denomination represented in the room. This word from the Lord would soon become a key declaration in every place I went. With passionate prayer, I would proclaim and release permission to burn over every person, young and old. The bindings of legalism and division broke like chains. We could almost hear the sound of shackles hitting the floor as the Lord declared, "Now fly! The cage is open. You are no longer bound. I give you permission to be wild for Me." The synergy of the generations came together, and I believe the mantles of pioneers who went before us fell upon those who were willing to give their lives to radical obedience to God's voice and Word. The torch wasn't just being passed; it was being grasped in unity. The hearts there were crying, "We will run this race together!"

I saw the hearts of the fathers turning back to the sons and the sons turning back to the fathers as they worshiped together in response to this heaven-sent permission. I began to realize this permission from heaven could be a demarcation point of the beginning of the greatest revival the world would ever see. It was a culmination of every movement and every pioneer of freedom in Him coming together—with a sound roaring from heaven as if the voices of the great cloud of witnesses were declaring, "Yes, *burn* for Jesus in purity, holiness, and freedom! We died so you might live unhindered to finish the work and see the fulfillment of the promises we have yet to see." It reminds me of the section of Scripture that tells the next generation to pick up the fallen mantles, so the sacrifices of the martyrs would not be in vain (see Heb. 11:37-40).

Tony Ramos, a missionary to the United States at IHOP Atlanta, shared his encouraging view of this generation.

Holy Dissatisfaction

There is a roar coming from the youth in America that has been silenced by the mundane, mediocre Christianity we have been used to for centuries. I have been a witness of the power of God marking the hearts of young revivalists who are Daniel and John the Baptist types, who have made it their goal to not give rest to their eyes until they find a place for the mighty one of Jacob in America and the nations.

For this is the generation the Lord was talking about when He talked about the generation of Jacob; those that will seek His face, and who will not give in to the woes of society and will take their places to see the injustices that have plagued the earth far too long be taken down for good (Ps. 24:6-8). They know it all depends on God, but the power is in their sacrifices of prayer and proclamations of faith in Jesus to turn the tide; they will risk it all to see the worth of Jesus known. How exciting! Wouldn't you be filled with such a flame in your heart if you knew who you were in Christ—if you really knew He loved you and gave you authority over the powers of the air to command angels and release the supernatural in your city?

- Tony Ramos, Missionary, IHOP Atlanta

I dream of the time when Christ is the head and we are submitted one to another without competition or dishonor, with one goal: to see Jesus be glorified on the earth. I dream of the time when the fivefold ministry carriers, the musicians and singers, the young and old intercessors, and the other various gifts holders can seamlessly submit to the Father—to do what He does, say what He says, and pray what He prays—as did Jesus. In that day, the young ones will learn from the wisdom and experience of the mature, and the mature will be awakened to dream with God by the fiery zeal and God-given vision in the young.

My dream is the dream of God that the prophecy fulfilled in Acts 2 would manifest in our generation—"old men dream dreams and the young men see visions" (see Acts 2:17)—and His Spirit would be poured out upon both men and women, and His sons and daughters would mature into pure prophetic accuracy. My dream is that this revival would defeat division in the church so the world might know the love of God and the salvation of Jesus Christ as described in John 17. I desire to see such reckless devotion in the body of Christ that the lost would rush to be saved and the Bridegroom would return for His longing—His spotless, unified bride.

Cry Out

> Mark me, Lord! I want to be marked with holy dissatisfaction. I thank You for all of the messengers who have gone before me. Thank You for those who are emerging now. Thank You for their prayers and work in the kingdom of God. Forgive me if I have not honored them well. I forgive them for where they were wrong. Lay upon me a mantle of honor, humility, and purity. May I be used in the ministry of reconciliation. Open up the heavens, release Your glory, and let Your kingdom come to earth. Make me a messenger of fire and love.

7
PURIFICATION AND OFFENSE

My face was soaked with tears, and my mascara was running. I had danced and worshiped my heart out for over an hour in front of the church, and I hadn't cared who saw me. I was making my way back to my seat to join my husband for the preaching portion of the service when this woman pulled me to the side and warned me, with disdain, "Young lady, as you mature in the Lord, that fire will go out, and you will come and go like the rest of us. Tone it down. You are provoking your husband. He's the spiritual leader of the home, not you. Listen to what I say and grow up!"

Permission to Burn

Several years had passed since I caught fire for the Lord. I had received tremendous healing. No one warned me that holy dissatisfaction would cause friction. Yet in that season, my flaming heart for God was tested and stretched by those closest to me. Family and relationships within my Christian community became increasingly difficult—more than I had ever expected. I was not mentally prepared for this purification process. I look back now and see how I was being sharpened and pressed deeper into God's heart. I learned how to pray through deep anguish and to love even when it hurt.

I believe everyone goes through these seasons in their walk with the Lord. I was zealous for the Lord, and even when I thought I was failing, the deep inner craving for more of Him continued to grow. I found my entire identity, purpose, and destiny in Him. Little did I know that the holy fire I lived in would offend some of the believers I looked to as mentors.

Will My Fire Go Out?

When I was rebuked for my extravagant worship, I was so confused by her words, but I made a commitment to the Lord in my heart that I would burn with passion and be on fire all the days of my life. But the comment somehow stayed with me. I wanted nothing more than for my husband to lead and to take the earth for Jesus with me. I had no idea the fire of God was offending the cold and lukewarm believers.

Jesus didn't come into the world to offend, but offense still came. He was called the rock of offense (see Isa. 28:16; Rom. 9:30-33). The offended people, most often religious leaders, justified their behavior because they hated the light

Purification and Offense

and burning that came with the message and person of Jesus. The Light of the world was a flame of pure fire, which exposed their double standards and compromised lifestyles. John talked about this at the beginning of his gospel.

> For God did not send the Son into the world to judge the world, but that the world might be saved through Him. He who believes in Him is not judged; he who does not believe has been judged already, because he has not believed in the name of the only begotten Son of God. This is the judgment, that the Light has come into the world, and men loved the darkness rather than the Light, for their deeds were evil. For everyone who does evil hates the Light, and does not come to the Light for fear that his deeds will be exposed.
>
> – John 3:17-20

This can be likened to the law of gravity. Gravity does not kill a man who jumps off a cliff. The man's rebellion against, and unbelief in, the law of gravity causes his death. Likewise, some people are offended by the light of Christ because they love the darkness that hides their evil deeds. Because the light exposes them, they retaliate against the purity of the love-sick lovers of Jesus—either out of ignorance or personal offense.

People who are rigid in religion spew hatred and offense in a more painful and ugly way. Often they unknowingly target the messengers of Jesus who are the most beautiful, pure, and free. They are in love with heaping theological debates and doctrines upon the necks of those who burn with freedom. The enemy works slyly through them, using their pain and jealousy. Many times,

Permission to Burn

such people use fear to sow seeds of doubt and trepidation into the minds and souls of zealous children of God, all while they are jumping into the darkness to hide the bitterness and hatred within their own hearts. They place weighty, religious yokes upon the necks of newly free believers, as Jesus said of the Pharisees of His day.

> Jesus spoke to the crowds and to His disciples, saying: "The scribes and the Pharisees have seated themselves in the chair of Moses; therefore all that they tell you, do and observe, but do not do according to their deeds; for they say things and do not do them. They tie up heavy burdens and lay them on men's shoulders, but they themselves are unwilling to move them with so much as a finger.
>
> But they do all their deeds to be noticed by men; for they broaden their phylacteries and lengthen the tassels of their garments. They love the place of honor at banquets and the chief seats in the synagogues, and respectful greetings in the market places, and being called Rabbi by men. But the greatest among you shall be your servant. Whoever exalts himself shall be humbled; and whoever humbles himself shall be exalted."
>
> – Matthew 23:1-12

Over the next few years, the enemy worked hard to use offensive and judgmental statements, like those of the lady at my church, to douse the love-sick fire in my heart. Abiding in prayer became an anchor for me. A daily focus of Scripture study and intercession was spent to guard my heart against bitterness, rejection, and rebellion.

Purification and Offense

The Fairy-Tale Marriage under Attack

Dissatisfaction is not always holy. There is a lifelong journey involved when walking in holiness and consistently growing hunger. The spiritual war became more intense as my marriage quickly came under attack. This Christian marriage suddenly was not manifesting like the world-changing fairy tale I dreamed it would be. We seemed to have two different visions for our family. In my mind, our destiny together would be to live as modern missionaries, to win the lost and release revival all over the earth by faith, but it seemed like my business-minded husband's dream was very different.

Well-meaning ladies told me the conflict was my issue to fix as a godly wife. The issue, as they saw it, was that I needed to be more submissive toward my husband. They told me I had to forget my dream and pick up his so we could be one. As the wife, this was my responsibility. If we were having problems, I was the problem. I was the one with the past. I was counseled to be a little more down to earth and do the "southern Christian family" kind of normal—not all this "be a flame upon the earth" kind of thing. It was as though being a flame was sinful and rebellious. However, I knew in my gut that the "southern thing" was religious, lukewarm living, as mentioned in Revelation 3:16.

For the next few years, intense debates came up over scriptural interpretation, doctrine, and gender roles. I was a tender yet strong-willed young lady in my twenties who had been through hell and back. My whole existence was for one purpose—to take the world for Jesus. Jesus had redeemed me and given back the education and life the enemy had tried to steal from me. He loved me and delivered me from all my sin and gave me an undeserved new life. I wasn't going down without a fight. At the same time, I longed for wisdom, and I wanted to remain teachable. But I had to learn the holy and humble part of being dissatisfied. I had to learn my identity was not in what I could do *for* God but in who I am *in* Him.

Looking back, I now see I was being sharpened. I felt like I was going to die, but I wanted to obey, even if it killed me. The cycles of fight, die, submit, fight, die, submit continued on and off for what seemed like forever. The truth is, I died a million deaths in that season. I died to my selfish ambition, and I learned how to really pray. The boundaries I learned in this season of intense conflict were, in some ways, wisdom, but in other ways, they were man-made walls. I had to identify what was God and what was false doctrine.

This passage from Ephesians 6 become my lifeline and helped me understand that fighting in the flesh would never accomplish anything:

> For our struggle is not against flesh and blood, but against the rulers, against the powers, against the world forces of this darkness, against the spiritual forces of wickedness in the heavenly places. Therefore, take up the full armor of God, so that you will be able to resist in the evil day, and having done everything, to stand firm. Stand firm therefore, having girded your loins with truth, and having put on the breastplate of righteousness, and having shod your feet with the preparation of the gospel of peace; in addition to all, taking up the shield of faith with which you will be able to extinguish all the flaming arrows of the evil one.

Purification and Offense

And take the helmet of salvation, and the sword of the Spirit, which is the word of God. With all prayer and petition pray at all times in the Spirit, and with this in view, be on the alert with all perseverance and petition for all the saints, and pray on my behalf, that utterance may be given to me in the opening of my mouth, to make known with boldness the mystery of the gospel, for which I am an ambassador in chains; that in proclaiming it I may speak boldly, as I ought to speak.

– Ephesians 6:12-20

The Rollercoaster Continues

During that season, I would intercede intensely and worship with extravagance during church on Sundays; but when I tried to tell others the beautiful things the Father had spoken to me, I received only rebukes. I was told by some that I was not hearing from God or I was too intense or I was just plain offensive. People also said the college ministry my husband and I led was a distraction to our marriage. Truthfully, it was a point of argument constantly. My husband just wanted normalcy, but I was still fighting in the spirit and sometimes in the physical for what I called my destiny.

Meanwhile, the ministry on campus was exploding. Fiery worshipers of all races and denominations would pack the room. These students were on fire. They came to our house to hear about the baptism of the Holy Spirit and fire and received like sponges. But they stayed late into the night a few days a week. The meetings on campus, on Tuesday nights, didn't start until 9 p.m. because of class schedules. Being fresh out of college, this was normal to me. I was used to late hours and long days of working a full-time job.

I didn't realize my late nights on the local campus a few days a week would be seen as neglecting the home, but I was regularly pulled aside and told I needed to stay home, quit ministering to the students, and stop fasting and praying all the time. My radical pursuit of God was "no earthly good" and was upsetting. Over and over, I was rebuked. Religiously, they said I was completely out of order.

Again, my heart broke. I hadn't grown up this way. Family life was a very important part of my dream, and it was woven beautifully into revival in my heart. I wrestled with whether the advice I was being given held truth. Did I truly need to adjust? But the question that still plagued my soul was why I was so offensive in my love-sick stupor. Why did it feel like the people who used to love my zeal for the Lord now want to kill it?

I wanted so desperately to be pleasing to the Lord and to my husband that I became less vocal and purposely restricted my rate of growth in the Lord. I started turning off the worship music and making sure my total focus was on him when he came home from work. I did this because someone had suggested to me that we had so much tension in our home because my relationship with God made him feel like less of a spiritual leader. Shortly after, I became pregnant with our first baby, and the ministry on campus came to a close. The only way I knew to fix our problems was to douse my own fire and focus more on making my family happy. I was trying to compartmentalize God into one box and family into another. This was a big mistake.

The harder I tried to make everyone happy with me, the more hopelessness began to set in. I felt as though I had to

Purification and Offense

hide my love-sick relationship with Jesus, as though I was having an affair. All this time, Daymon knew little of the seeds of religious confusion that were being sown into his fiery wife. It seemed all of hell fought to divide us. I was sad and deeply wounded, and I cried a lot in prayer and felt alone.

My joy was almost gone, and I felt like I was in a cage. Daymon was suffering as well. Had he known the counsel I was getting, he would have called it ridiculous. My husband is a strong man of God, and he would have been angry to find I was admonished concerning my zeal for God. He was not that shallow. Honestly, the opposite was true. He fell in love with me as a fiery, love-sick worshiper and wanted her back. Even in all our debates, he never wanted me to quench the flames in my heart. Amid the storms, we were sharpening and humbling one another. We would come to know the Lord had joined together a dream team. He is a wise, rock-solid, kingdom-minded businessman and I am a fiery prophetic messenger.

Beloved, as we grow in our passion for the Lord, trials will come, and the offense will try to douse the purity of the flames in our hungry hearts. As I mentioned, our war is not against flesh and blood (Ephesians 6:12). The people who seem to be at odds with us are not our enemies. The enemy is Satan, and he is not after our ministries or careers. He is after our intimacy with God, our purity, and our tenderness to the Holy Spirit. Ultimately, he wants our generational legacy—our family.

Satan wants to destroy God's love in your heart. He wants to get you offended and self-seeking. He wants you bitter and rebellious or timid, legalistic, silent, and hopeless.

Permission to Burn

God aims to mature us, humble us, and sharpen us. Our Father wants to teach us to pray and to love sacrificially, especially during the times of trial. As in the story of Joseph and his family (in Genesis 50), God will take our pit experience and use it to position our entire household for greatness. "Joseph replied, 'Do not be afraid. Am I in the place of God? As for you, what you intended against me for evil, God intended for good, in order to accomplish a day like this—to preserve the lives of many people. Therefore do not be afraid. I will provide for you and your little ones.' So Joseph reassured his brothers and spoke kindly to them" (Genesis 50:18-21).

Intimacy with God cannot be compartmentalized. Your zeal may upset some people, but the dream will come to pass.

The journey is more important than the destination. The more we mature in our walk with the Lord, the more we realize how much we need to grow up. Living on fire is not about proving our zeal or rightness before others. It's about being a humble, pure son or daughter and allowing the overflow of His presence to minister to others daily. Through it all, we experience the faithfulness of God. What the enemy intends for evil in our lives, God wants to use to deliver us and our families. I am convinced that true revival will manifest as we become family on fire.

Pray!

> If revival is family on fire, then open my eyes to Your work in our hearts. I want my entire family to experience the burning passion in my heart. Forgive me for my responses of offense or self-righteousness when I came under attack. Holy Spirit, deliver me from roots of rejection,

abandonment, offense, and bitterness. Heal and restore my closest relationships.

May I always be tender to Your voice and see others the way You see them. I realize that people can be like tools in Your hands, used to sharpen me and mature me. While the enemy was trying to quench my fire, You, Lord, had plans to prosper me and to give my family and me a hope and a future. Help me to never hide my zealous love for You and Your kingdom, but use it to bring awakening to others. Help me to walk in peace and love, even while under attack. I receive a fresh anointing to walk boldly before God and man.

8

THE DREAM OF KINGDOM UNITY

So many people think unity means everyone compromising to get along and do an event together. That is not unity. That is tolerance. God the Father is the true builder of unity. "Unless the Lord builds the house, those who build it labor in vain" (Psalm 127:1 ESV), and Jesus is the chief cornerstone of unity.

Permission to Burn

Many years passed, and the marriage battles greatly subsided. Daymon and I learned how to communicate with one another, keep Jesus at the center of our marriage, and stop assuming we knew it all. Once again, my fire began burning more intensely, but by this time, I had grown in maturity and wisdom. We had three little girls and had endured many pains and victories, which had bonded us together. At one point, Daymon laid his hands on my head and blessed me to do and be all that God placed within me. He gave me permission to burn. We were far from perfect, but we had finally recognized the beauty in one another. I filled our house with prayer and worship after the Lord broke me free from being squashed by the spirit of religion, and this brought us into massive redemption.

Often, God walks with us through personal battles to purify, stretch, and sharpen us enough to handle regional, national, and even worldwide spiritual battles. God really does work everything out for the good of those who love Him and are called according to His purposes. He does not enjoy our pain or even bring it on us, but He uses it beautifully to "stretch out our tent pegs." Nothing is wasted when placed in the hands of God. In all the personal times of pressing, we had no idea the Lord was preparing us to take national and even worldwide territory for His glory. We were just trying to survive, be leaders in a church, be married, and raise a godly family.

The Beauty from the Pressing

The FireHouse Prayer Furnace launched an event in February of 2016 that beautifully ignited many people to burn, but after the excitement faded, we faced major backlash from the enemy. The move of God that took

The Dream of Kingdom Unity

place that weekend in February was supposed to be the kickoff of a dream in the heart of God—a dream that the prayer and revival hub would become a base that hosted His presence, a place many would call home and others would travel to quarterly to be refreshed, ignited with the fire of God, and sent back out into all the world. But it didn't take long for the enemy to send division among the people who came from so many different backgrounds.

The blissful ministry honeymoon period ended, and again the fiery passion for holiness and purity caused offense to arise. John Bevere wrote a book about this called *The Bait of Satan*. I believe this title about offense is true. At the same time, Jesus was called the rock of offense.

When the fire of God brings offense, we must know He is going to make something beautiful come out of what seems to be causing people to stumble over one another. Purity comes when the fire burns hot. Consider this passage, "He will sit as a refiner and purifier of silver, he will purify the Levites and refine them like gold and silver. The Lord will have men who bring offerings in righteousness" (Mal. 3:3 NIV).

It is true that we want unity, and this divisive, backbiting, accusing spirit is a demonic phenomenon that we must defeat. But it will only be purged by holy fire. If we want to see the promise of awakening fulfilled in our time, we must be a generation that embraces the fire. Events are amazing, but God wants unity to reign in the body of Christ, and He wants His word to go forth with sustainability in His people. The unity Jesus spoke of (in John 17) will not come in any way other than by embracing the fire and glory of our amazing, fiery, holy, pure, and just God.

Permission to Burn

His will and His kingdom will come when we ask for it, and then we will find ourselves challenged to align with His vision. Jesus became a rock of offense because the religious leaders would not embrace the fire to purify their hearts and align themselves with Him. So many people think unity means everyone compromising to get along and do an event together. That is not unity. That is tolerance. That is building the Tower of Babel (see Gen. 11:1-9). God the Father is the true builder of unity. Psalm 127:1 (ESV) says, "Unless the Lord builds the house, those who build it labor in vain," and Jesus is the chief cornerstone of unity.

The "permission to burn," message is for all ages. This message from the throne room of heaven has deeply affected many, and it always challenges people in every area of their lives after they receive the fiery impartation. I always give a loving warning that people must prepare for their hearts to be purified and for their eyes to be opened. I tell them, "When you go home, remember to run *to* the fire and not away from it, for the rock of offence will surely come." That is exactly what a precious woman, Jessica, who sent me this testimony, discovered.

> Depending on how you grew up, this word could have a positive or a negative connotation for you. As an adult, it's not really something you think about needing. You are an adult. You finally don't need permission. The problem is, for most of us, that is just not true.
>
> The Lord brought me out of a world of turmoil and chaos, where walking on eggshells was the norm. What I have encountered in the years I've spent following Tammie's ministry was first the

The Dream of Kingdom Unity

words "permission granted." The Lord moved so powerfully in me when I heard this message. Hearing His yes first became my yes to Him forever. In this truth was the transition of salvation, acceptance, identity, and the love of the Father from my head to my heart. In that place, I began to see Jesus for who He really is biblically, and so much more personally. The beauty of walking out this faith journey with Him and becoming like Him was much less concept and far more a reality. The grace to surrender to the Potter was born.

When "permission to burn" came forth, an explosion of hunger by the power of Holy Spirit began to give words to the awe and transformation I had been experiencing. Cleansing, grieving, healing tears in response to the revealing and cutting away as I continually submitted myself before the Lord with my yes gave way to a new lens. It was permission for me to be the person He created me to be—His original intention for me—to emerge a truly new creation, accepted in the beloved, embedded in the vine, and shining for His glory. The Firehouse has always been a place of freedom and holy passion that honors and fears the Lord. I have formed bonds that have challenged and blessed me in ways I may not ever fully understand, and I experienced the joy of community all of us were created for.

My prayer is that this same process would be embraced by people caught up in legalism and man-made traditions, by those in caves being called out, and by those in the wilderness. I pray a new generation will be raised up without the shackles this world tries to impose on us. It is indeed time for the body to burn for her Groom.

Here is another example from a man, Alan, of how transformational the "permission to burn" message is.

> My personal experience with the "permission to burn" message has truly been a life-changing journey. It took me from a place of being performance driven with my spiritual gifts to a place of just existing in God's presence and finding peace and joy in simply being with Daddy God. From that place of allowing myself to thrive as a son, I have found so much of what I had once strived for begin to come forth in my life without any effort on my part. I just had to experience the Father's joy in imparting more of Himself and His character into my life. I am thoroughly thankful and blessed for Tammie and the "permission to burn" culture and revelation.

I believe God wants to have a fiery home base like this in every nation and every city across the earth. He wants places that host His presence, where people run to the beauty of His fire and glory, not away from it. The dream of my heart is that I will be used as His trumpet to blow the living message of His beauty. I long for a people to arise who will allow Him to build His house in their cities (see Ps. 127). These will be places of His presence, where the body of Christ can come together in burning fellowship with Him. The cycles of division and territorial competition among the brethren must cease. However, this can only take place as we lay down our rights to territory and our man-made blueprints. It all belongs to the

The Dream of Kingdom Unity

Bridegroom, and He longs to reign with His *spotless* bride, but we are a broken, immature, offended, competing, cannibalizing body. We must abide in prayer, seeking to see though His eyes and grasp His vision.

I believe small groups of people—I call them pockets of fire—who hunger for the manifestation of God's dream and heavenly blueprint, exist all over the world. Right now, these remnant groups are maintaining this kind of pure fire. They are hidden and longing to live consecrated lives. These hidden ones do not just go to church and sit in a pew on Sunday mornings. They give themselves to the lifestyle of prayer. One of the biggest phenomena in the westernized church right now is that people are leaving the traditional Sunday morning church meetings so they can burn and worship unhindered by systems and agendas. I do not necessarily believe leaving one's church is always the answer, but I do think God is leading this migration of the sons and daughters to find the pastors and fivefold ministry leaders who have given their lives to intercession, the study of the Word of God, and the hosting of the presence of God in purity.

Many of these people who are leaving organized, systematic churches don't hate the church; they love it so much that they meet in intercession for the true *ekklesia* to arise and be restored. They cry out for bindings of darkness' doctrines of demons; and controlling, man-made religion to be no more. These pockets are the true *ekklesia* that Jesus spoke to Peter about—the living stones (the people who make up true *ekklesia*) who are being built upon the chief cornerstone (Jesus), whom the builders (the religious) rejected.

These people don't want their ministries to look like Christian businesses and Christian entertainment centers.

Permission to Burn

These pioneers hunger for 24-7 hubs of His presence and places His people can call home. They hunger for true biblical communion together as family with the Father, Son, and Holy Spirit. These places will arise and be places of true equipping and sending. Those who come out of these places will also come back to them. They won't try to bust out in rebellion, because they won't have to. They don't have to fear being held back from their God-given destiny. These humble leaders will release God's permission of true burning all over the nations, and they will awaken the hearts of the nations to the family in Christ. They will demonstrate how to impact the world while not conforming to it, and model consecration and zealous love.

God's desire is to raise up sons and daughters and mothers and fathers who will burn for Jesus no matter where they are and no matter what they're doing, as a lifestyle. We learn to become thankful for the trials, because they brought us to the point of seeing what He sees and believing Him for the great harvest that is coming. The Father is responding to the groan in hearts all over the earth to give sons and daughters a place called home. This generation desperately needs examples of true family.

Dreams and visions will be made manifest in communities of fiery ones who belong to the Father. Hearts and lives will be knit together by the true love of Christ. The Lord desires artists of all kinds to be free to manifest the heart of the Father. Thinkers are to be welcome to wrestle with the things of God, so they can walk out with a limp, like Jacob, knowing they encountered the true, living God. Poets are welcome to express His heart in these furnaces of the Father's love. Quiet whisperers are invited to meditate on the things of

The Dream of Kingdom Unity

the Lord and not have to say a word. Singers can sing the songs of the Lord. Musicians can play the sounds of heaven. Writers can pen the words of revelation in sweet moments of worship. Prayer warriors can pray the depths of their anguish and dance in the extravagant joy of the Lord.

Evangelists can be radical about winning souls. Teachers can teach the prophetic utterances that the prophets prophesied. The apostles are welcome to give their lives to prayer, fasting, and studying the Word of the Lord, so that when they strategize, they have the pure, heavenly blueprint, not a man-made, Tower-of-Babel type of political strategy. The pastoring shepherds can be free to nurture the broken and care for the widows and the orphans. Christ is to be the head in these places. He is the building. His people function as His body, and He is in control.

Isaiah 35 talks about a river in the wilderness that nourishes the land, creating a place that no beast can devour.

> The wilderness and the desert will be glad, and the Arabah will rejoice and blossom; like the crocus it will blossom profusely and rejoice with rejoicing and shout of joy. The glory of Lebanon will be given to it, the majesty of Carmel and Sharon. They will see the glory of the Lord, the majesty of our God.
> Encourage the exhausted and strengthen the feeble. Say to those with anxious heart, "Take courage, fear not. Behold, your God will come with vengeance; the recompense of God will come, but He will save you." Then the eyes of the blind will be opened and the ears of the deaf will be unstopped.

> Then the lame will leap like a deer, and the tongue of the mute will shout for joy. For waters will break forth in the wilderness and streams in the Arabah. The scorched land will become a pool and the thirsty ground springs of water; in the haunt of jackals, its resting place, grass becomes reeds and rushes.
>
> A highway will be there, a roadway, and it will be called the Highway of Holiness. The unclean will not travel on it, but it will be for him who walks that way, and fools will not wander on it. No lion will be there, nor will any vicious beast go up on it; these will not be found there. But the redeemed will walk there, and the ransomed of the Lord will return and come with joyful shouting to Zion, with everlasting joy upon their heads. They will find gladness and joy, and sorrow and sighing will flee away.
>
> – Isaiah 35:1-10

I believe that if we truly allow the Spirit of God to be in control, submitting one to another and to Him, the gates of hell (including any spirit of division or Jezebel) cannot prevail against us. The house of the Lord is home. It is the beloved place of hiddenness in the wilderness, which is safe from the destroyer. It is the place where the sons and daughters learn the deeper identity of being the bride of Christ. Therein is the foundation to believe that being pure doers of the Word is more than permissible—it's a reason for existing.

The Dream of Kingdom Unity

Hosting His Presence

This may sound like a utopian dream, but it's the dream of God to have a place where we have dominion but we trust Him to be in control. He died for our freedom to burn for Him and to be holy as He is holy. Our hearts' cry should be the same as the cry of the heart of King David: "One thing I have asked from the Lord, that I shall seek: that I may dwell in the house of the Lord all the days of my life" (Ps. 27:4).

Before we moved to Clemson, God asked me this simple question, *Are you willing to host My presence?* That's where it all started—being willing to host Him and let Him lead; only doing what He does and saying what He says; letting the songs, prayers, and messages come from heaven; and allowing the burning ones to burn. Even more than that, I learned to be the temple of His presence and His house. I learned that it's not so much about a building or a ministry rather than just being with Him and becoming the sign and the wonder.

I learned that He wants me to be the burning bush that's not consumed. This reality became the message and hunger of my life—not to build a ministry but to stay seated with Him in heavenly places as a lifestyle and to invite others to come up and sit in that place (see Eph. 2:6). I want to invite others to pray what He is praying and do what He is doing, to burn with me and not just watch me burn.

King David was wrecked with the desire to build a place where the presence of God could dwell among His people. His whole life was ruined with this desire. He went through a lot to lean into the fact that "the one thing" was not about a building but a dwelling place—"One thing I ask from the Lord, this only do I seek: that I may dwell in the house of the Lord all the days of my life, to gaze on the beauty of the Lord and seek him in his temple" (Ps. 27:4 NIV).

I've been wrecked with a dream too—to see a mass harvest of souls fill stadiums and auditoriums around the world, but only if they are willing to burn for Jesus all the days of their lives. I want them to come only if they will make the main thing the one thing. Is it possible that we could fill stadiums and impart hunger for true, lifelong burning? Gathering in masses and having a good day together is not good enough. Even having a bunch of people say the sinner's prayer in response to a good message is not good enough to satisfy the burning desire in the guts of nations. The prophet Haggai said, "Thus saith the Lord of hosts; Yet once, it is a little while, and I will shake the heavens, and the earth, and the sea, and the dry land; and I will shake all nations, and the desire of all nations shall come: and I will fill this house with glory, saith the Lord of hosts" (Haggai 2:6-7 KJV).

What if the heavens and earth shook and the nations quaked into a spiritual awakening? What if the sleeping global bride realized her burning desire for Jesus and for His glory to cover the earth through her? What if people gathered together in hunger for the God-Man, Jesus? What if this awakening caused Him to come down and fill people groups with His glory? I believe a massive harvest would break forth, and the ripple effect would be that Israel would burn with jealousy and be saved.

How amazing would it be to see God fill stadiums with a harvest of souls who were immediately marked with hunger such as we have never seen? People would leave with a holy hunger that never leaves, and a generation

THE DREAM OF KINGDOM UNITY

would become the dwelling place of the Lord as a lifestyle. We must fast and pray for a convergence of glory, fire, and hunger that will mark the massive remnant to birth a generation that burns with unquenchable, holy fire.

A convergence is coming in which the different streams in the body of Christ will cause the Father to release the Son, the Bridegroom, to split the skies in return for His love-sick, pure, and spotless bride. I believe heaven has granted us permission to burn because this is His longing as well. I believe He is igniting our hearts to get past the ideas of "the business" of ministry, or even the business of the world, and to come back to our first love—to simply burn for Him and be about His business.

THE CRY OF HIS HEART

At the end of Revelation, John records these words, which show us the cry of God's heart: The Spirit and the bride say, "Come!" And let the one who hears say, "Come!" Let the one who is thirsty come; and let the one who wishes take the free gift of the water of life" (Revelation 22:17 NIV).

I believe God is crying out to us,

> Come home, beloved one! You have permission from heaven to burn with My pure fire, to be free and to purely love what I love and hate what I hate. You have permission to rest from human pressure and simply be the son or daughter I created you to be. Find a place called home in Me. Rest, you weary one, and sit down in My lap. I will lead you, and you will find where My presence dwells. I dwell among the broken yet pure-hearted people who long for Me and only Me.

> I challenge you to find mothers and fathers in the faith who are in love with Me and ask them how they are still on fire at their age. They are out there, My beloved one. If your fire has grown cold, let Me, your Daddy in heaven, heal your wounds of disappointment and fill you again. Connect with those zealous sons and daughters who challenge you. I have placed them in your life to fuel your fire. Let them! You need them and they need you. I want you to dream with Me again."

Even now, I see babies leaping in the wombs of older, barren intercessors as the young ones are arising. The young ones carrying this movement are the answer to the prayers of the older generations. We must fan their flames and pour our God dreams out on them, because our dreams will awaken their vision. As the Scripture says, "Where there is no vision, the people perish" (Prov. 29:18 KJV). I believe the Elizabeths (older prophets and intercessors) and Marys (younger prophets and intercessors) coming together will birth the convergence of the John the Baptist (pioneer) and Jesus (evangelism with power) movements.

Massive redemption from past trials, and hungering for His eyes to see how He is moving, is the key to filling houses, buildings, and arenas with the glory of the Lord. Reconciliation is found in the presence of the Lord among a people who have been gripped with the one desire to look at the man Jesus. Unity is more than agreeing with people who are like us. Unity is being transformed into His likeness and enjoying the many facets of His glory that shine through diverse people.

The Dream of Kingdom Unity

Pray!

Encounter me with your beauty, Jesus. Make me to crave Your presence alone. Fix my eyes on You, the author and finisher of my faith. I want to see others the way You see them. I want to connect with the global bride as I become a personal host for Your presence. I want to ooze love and honor. In my region, I want to be a safe place for Your presence to dwell. I have a burning in my soul to know You and to be known by You. Create in me a burning for the world to encounter Your beauty. Make me a bold yet humble messenger.

9
Permission to Go

Therefore, go and make disciples of all nations, baptizing them in the name of the Father and of the Son and of the Holy Spirit.
— Matthew 28:19 NIV

Permission to Burn

Maria looked at me and began to cry. I was shocked and I prayed under my breath. My friends and I had spent a few hours in intercession and equipping our team for an inner-city outreach. In my arms was a box that contained a turkey and all the fixings. I had read over the little pamphlet ten times before we went out. I was very nervous, but the teachings in the brochure were seared into my heart. *Jesus is to be on the throne of your life.* That was a personal longing.

The butterflies in my stomach intensified, as this was my first outreach experience. I sat on the old sofa in Maria's home, quietly praying and observing as someone else read the pamphlet to her in English. The problem was, she didn't speak English; she was confused. Suddenly the atmosphere in the home shifted from confusion to clarity. It felt as though the Lord Himself walked into the room and took over my mouth. I thought I was whispering prayers in English, but Maria looked at me as my teammate read. She heard me and thought I was interpreting. Her eyes darted from the gospel brochure and then back to me. Tears began to stream down her face. She shouted, "Si, Jesus! Si, Jesus!" She was healed of back pain and accepted Jesus as her savior. Maria wept and rejoiced, and so did we! God saved and healed Maria. He sealed a passion for power and evangelism in our team. We were not just doing an outreach anymore, we became witnesses. After that day, my friends and I were hooked on fasting, prayer, and being used by God. Unfortunately, it would not be long until we got in trouble back home for our zeal to hit the streets. A few local church members were embarrassed and told the pastor that we were out of order and untrained. They wanted us to be stopped.

Permission to Go

We were in good company though. Peter and John ran into the same problem.

> As they observed the confidence of Peter and John and understood that they were uneducated and untrained men, they were amazed, and began to recognize them as having been with Jesus. And seeing the man who had been healed standing with them, they had nothing to say in reply. But when they had ordered them to leave the Council, they began to confer with one another, saying, "What shall we do with these men? For the fact that a noteworthy miracle has taken place through them is apparent to all who live in Jerusalem, and we cannot deny it. "But so that it will not spread any further among the people, let us warn them to speak no longer to any man in this name." And when they had summoned them, they commanded them not to speak or teach at all in the name of Jesus.
>
> – Acts 4:13-17

What is it about being untrained and uneducated that ruffles the feathers of the trained and educated? Training and education are very valuable until we become puffed up and treated like gods. Ordinary people who are being used by the supernatural power of God should cause us to marvel at the Lord. Naturally, those with higher education could teach the depths of the Scriptures and train others in maturity and tact. The Lord loves using what seems foolish to the world to confound the wise. More glory shines on Jesus when people can boast in Him alone. The trained and untrained would work beautifully together to reach the whole earth if their zeal and wisdom could humbly converge.

Peter and John had been with Jesus, and that was evident (v.13). What a compliment, right? Not so much to the religious leaders. Distorted religion craves control of others instead of giving them freedom and release. Unfortunately, there was no longing in their hearts to celebrate the wonder of a healed man. Nor was there a desire to learn from the apostles. Their hearts were hardened. They wanted one thing—to silence and control the wild ones. They loved the man-made traditions and the religious system that allowed only the elite to represent God.

As modern-day leaders, we must remain tender to the Lord and know our own hearts. If we are not aware that our seminary training is dung in light of the glory of the Lord, we could make the same mistake.

Most denominations favor the Great Commission Scriptures, preaching and teaching them regularly. Sadly, many leaders of the westernized church struggle to obey these passages. Even evangelistic outreach within many churches is sometimes lacking. The struggle to release members, especially their youth, to go illuminates an inner war. It is especially hard when fiery ones are hungry to be equipped at other ministry locations. Leaders often don't mind sending their people to conferences and meetings to ignite their fire for Jesus, but when those people come back with a vision from heaven, leaders often pour water on their holy flames by telling them to calm down, get back into the home-church culture, and do secular life.

Often, zealous young believers know they need training and don't want to rebel at all. Most are not trying to go into full-time missions or ministry without that

Permission to Go

foundation. They are hungry. They want a strong foundation; they desperately want to grow. At the same time, they are overflowing with excitement and the revelation that Jesus is the answer to everything. This is the perfect time for discipleship and for releasing them into the freedom of sharing Jesus with anyone who will listen. Unfortunately, many leaders see that zeal as a danger, when it is really the Lord stirring these new believers with His fire. Their passion would rightly be used to stoke the inner flames of the whole church.

For some reason, many leaders feel they must throttle those who desire to go and preach the good news, especially when the power of God is moving through them. They give reasons to tighten the grip that sound very spiritual. "So and so is not ready," or, "He needs to be better equipped, and we can do that here at our church," or, "She must have more of a foundation before she shares the gospel." Many zealous young believers want the opportunity to grow in a different church or ministry, but their leaders say, "You are needed here in our church," or, "Your gifting is only for our city." We do not realize that new church environments, and the equipping programs there, are precisely where the Lord wants to send them.

Sending is imperative to furthering the kingdom of heaven. The word "go" is written 1,542 times in Scripture. The disciples of Jesus were equipped daily as they walked with Jesus; they were sent out by Him within a tiny window of time. Many leaders would think it is best to hold people in the four walls of the building for ten to twenty years, but Jesus was sending people out with nothing but the clothes on their backs to preach, heal, raise the dead, and cast out demons (Mark 6:7-12). And when they thought He had just begun teaching them how to express the kingdom, He died on a cross, gave them His Spirit, and told them to do greater things than He did (John 16:7).

> He summoned the twelve and began to send them out in pairs, and gave them authority over the unclean spirits; and He instructed them that they should take nothing for their journey, except a mere staff—no bread, no bag, no money in their belt— but to wear sandals; and He added, "Do not put on two tunics." And He said to them, "Wherever you enter a house, stay there until you leave town. "Any place that does not receive you or listen to you, as you go out from there, shake the dust off the soles of your feet for a testimony against them." They went out and preached that men should repent. And they were casting out many demons and were anointing with oil many sick people and healing them."
>
> - Mark 6:7-12

Jesus's leadership method is circular in the way it never ends. In Scripture, we see him in relationship-based discipleship—modeling the life lesson, sending out, correcting, recommissioning, and more relationship, more teaching, more correcting, leading to more sending and so on. In Luke's account, the disciples came back excited about the demons knowing the authority of Jesus's name through them (Luke 10:17-21). I can see the delight in Jesus's eyes. He was so overjoyed at this moment. But at the same time, he didn't want them to lose the humility of heart. He wanted them to understand the bigger picture. Jesus admonished them to celebrate not in the power of God through them but that their names are written in the Lamb's book of life. He is a fantastic leader and a spiritual

Father. He always keeps eternity with Him as the central focus of the heart.

> The seventy returned with joy, saying, "Lord, even the demons are subject to us in Your name." And He said to them, "I was watching Satan fall from heaven like lightning. "Behold, I have given you authority to tread on serpents and scorpions, and over all the power of the enemy, and nothing will injure you. "Nevertheless do not rejoice in this, that the spirits are subject to you, but rejoice that your names are recorded in heaven."
>
> At that very time He rejoiced greatly in the Holy Spirit, and said, "I praise You, O Father, Lord of heaven and earth, that You have hidden these things from the wise and intelligent and have revealed them to infants. Yes, Father, for this way was well-pleasing in Your sight.
>
> – Luke 10:17-21

It is essential to teach, rebuke, edify, and equip. There is a way to strike the right balance in giving this generation a sure foundation to sustain burning throughout their lives. As ministers, we must make it a core value to remember that the purpose of ministry is to launch people into all the world with sustainable fire and to keep eternity with Jesus as the central focus. If we do well, we reach a point where we must release someone to go. This is emotionally difficult when we are very close to the son or daughter. We have invested dearly in their lives. Their desire to be launched into another area or another nation challenges us. That's what we live for, so bring on the challenge, right?

Permission to Burn

May each heart confrontation develop a more exceptional ability to love and mentor like Jesus. No leader wants to relinquish a hungry young person when his or her church is in such desperate need of that fire, yet Jesus not only released his disciples to go, but He expressed His own plan to go away. "But because I have said these things to you, sorrow has filled your heart. But I tell you the truth, it is to your advantage that I go away; for if I do not go away, the Helper will not come to you; but if I go, I will send Him to you" (John 16:6-7). "Going away" does not equate rejecting or abandoning relationships in the kingdom of heaven. Releasing in a season of transition looks more like a promotion for the sons and daughters of God. But if it feels painful or confusing, we are in good company. Jesus further revealed His plan to Peter and the others. In their minds, His timing and method were awful. The ways of the kingdom of God seem upside down to those of human reasoning. Let's take a look at this narrative.

> From that time on Jesus began to show His disciples that He must go to Jerusalem and suffer many things at the hands of the elders, chief priests, and scribes, and that He must be killed and on the third day be raised to life. Peter took Him aside and began to rebuke Him. "Far be it from You, Lord!" he said. "This shall never happen to You!" But Jesus turned and said to Peter, "Get behind Me, Satan! You are a stumbling block to Me. For you do not have in mind the things of God, but the things of men."
>
> – Matthew 16:21-23

Permission to Go

In the emotional realm, we are often like Peter. We want to stop what we don't understand. We must approach our position of leadership with much prayer, fasting, and discernment. How willing are we to lead like Jesus? The struggle to decrease like John the Baptist, or lay down our lives like Jesus, or simply to release spiritual sons and daughters is something to ponder.

Giving others permission to go is much like the moment when biological sons and daughters grow up and suddenly fall in love and want to get married, have children, and live the lives we have raised them to live. Or when they visit a college across the country and are compelled to move away so they can be equipped to begin their dream careers. As parents, we have groomed them for this. It means we have done well. But that doesn't make it easy.

Statistically, the parents of this generation tend to be afraid of releasing their children who are genuinely ready to go into the world. There is a lost and jaded world out there. Many say this generation is just not prepared. They are so immature. Daily, people are putting down the millennial generation for their laziness and their lack of commitment and focus. They are called dreamers who have no ambition or promise to fulfill their dreams; however, statistics show a generation of leaders and parents is to blame. Some parents are hoverers or helicopter parents who are overly attached and fearful of releasing their children into the real world. Often, the parents of this generation are partially responsible for the lack of drive in their children, because they have done everything for them and have not allowed them to venture out and fail a few times without experiencing pain. Others bash them for failure, and still, some sugarcoat it too much. Where are those who allow them freedom to fail with loving correction?

We must teach that mistakes, pain, and correction can lead to eventual success and healing. Many parents and leaders are on the extreme fringes. Kids have been shown to dream big but not how to persevere. Overprotection has held back these dreamers from accomplishing their destinies. The self-esteem of many millennials has been overinflated in that they are encouraged to dream bigger but never invited to self-correct, nor have they been taught that constructive criticism is a blessing when they fail. As the humanistic culture streams into the church, church leaders often fall into the same cycles—struggling to give people the freedom to go or freedom to fail and learn from the failures. We have lost the art of training.

Of my three children, none could walk without first falling. Imagine if, as they were learning to walk, I had told them, "That's okay. It's best to just keep crawling. It's safer down there." I would have condemned them to a life of crawling because they were prevented from walking at that moment. I would've crippled them for life. If I had not allowed them the freedom to fall as they learned to walk, I would have hindered their lives.

My point is that as leaders, it's time to teach, train, equip, and then release this generation to go, even if it means they fall. They will get back up and learn from their mistakes if we are there to correct them with truth in love. If they begin to run too fast and do amazing things for the Lord, and we think they are not ready, it's okay; they will always come back home, because the ones who love them encourage them to go and to never quit. We must remember that they belong to the Lord, not us. He is the great shepherd and Father.

PERMISSION TO GO

TRAINING IS ESSENTIAL

Beloved, let us begin the movement of hands-on training, equipping, and sending. Rick Joyner of Morning Star Ministries in Charlotte, North Carolina, said that preparation for awakening is key to sustaining it. He expressed that "training is not just teaching people, but training is when you actually take them out to do it. The Lord sent them out two by two (in Luke 10), and they did what they were being taught." As an air force instructor, Rick took men and women out to fly airplanes under supervision. They had to prepare. Much of the church's focus is on teaching and equipping. Training is the missing element that allows for supervised times of failure and correction, and these lead to powerful times of deployment.

The words of Jesus's commission are to make disciples of all nations (see Mark 16:15). Sending believers to go into all the world to preach the gospel to every creature is a vital part of seeing the third great awakening take place. "He said to them, 'Go into all the world and preach the gospel to all creation. He who has believed and has been baptized shall be saved; but he who has disbelieved shall be condemned'" (Mark 16:15-16). I see a movement emerging in which training and instruction go hand in hand, in which disappointment dissolves and the passion returns.

It is important to note that just before Jesus commissioned His disciples, He came to them and corrected them for their feelings of inadequacy and lack of faith. "Afterward He appeared to the eleven themselves as they were reclining at the table; and He reproached them for their unbelief and hardness of heart, because they had not believed those who had seen Him after He had risen"

Permission to Burn

(Mark 16:14). It appears Jesus rebuked them because *they did not understand*. But interestingly, in response to this unbelief, He commanded them to go. Who rebukes someone for rejecting a messenger, then commands them to go out and represent him?

Jesus's leadership is impressive. He equated their sitting and eating with unbelief and hardness of heart. The fact that they were sitting and doing what they'd always done exposed the disbelief in their hearts. Some leaders would call this failure and see the disciples as being in need of a sabbatical and further instruction. Jesus's discipline is to awaken hearts and prepare them for fiery deployment. An encounter with Jesus should ever compel true believers to go and tell the whole world about Him. Essentially, Jesus was saying, "How could you receive a message from those who encountered Me in my resurrected body and continue sitting around, hanging out, and scarfing down food? Now that you see, go! A lost and dying world is waiting."

My question is, do we really believe? If we really believed, wouldn't we be absolutely elated to go and be messengers, train messengers, and deploy messengers of the Lord into the fields that are white for harvest? We must ask ourselves if we are an unbelieving church. Have we fallen away from our first love? If we have, that's why He is showing up right now to awaken and realign our hearts with His. If the disciples who walked with Jesus in the flesh, and who received the message of His resurrection from their friends, could fall into the trap of unbelief, then how much more should we check our hearts when we begin to delay sons and daughters who are compelled to go?

Permission to Go

Ekballo: The Compelling

Awakening is more than lingo. Have you ever been in a deep sleep and heard a loud noise in the night? Your heart races. *Is someone invading my home?* If you are like me, you suddenly sit up in your bed. Your feet launch out and onto the floor. Seemingly intuitively, you make a plan of action to protect your sleeping loved ones. You have been awakened and you must respond to the inner urgency.

When Jesus awakens desire in a believer to go into the world as a burning messenger, there is a strong inner compulsion present. The Greek word *ekballo* is used in Scripture when Jesus drove out demons by the finger of God. *Ekballo* is also translated as "send" when Jesus said to pray that the Lord of the harvest would send forth laborers into the fields (see Matt. 9:38; Luke 10:2). As Lou Engle says, "When Jesus *ekballos* demons, demons must leave. When Jesus *ekballos* laborers, evangelists and missionaries must go out" (Mission Frontiers, Jul/Aug 2014). *Ekballo* means to violently cast out. It is a supernatural compulsion that God places in the DNA of the new believer to go and preach.

Have you ever felt possessed by God to tell of His beauty? Beloved, if you haven't, get around the throne of God. All Christians are saved to maintain a fire in their bones that demands release. When the Word of the Lord stirs as we encounter Jesus, we feel a compulsion from heaven to go and preach the gospel to every creature. The salvation of the world depends on this spiritual phenomenon. "He who has believed and has been baptized shall be saved; but he who has disbelieved shall be condemned" (Mark 16:16). Preventing a believer who is compelled to go from going opposes God. If we choose to harden our hearts against His prodding, we grieve His

Permission to Burn

Spirit. That can be hard to swallow, but it's based on the words of Jesus: "He reproached them for their unbelief and hardness of heart, because they had not believed those who had seen Him after He had risen" (Mark 16:14).

Christ in us is the hope of glory (Colossians 1:27). Supernatural urging has multiple layers. It's to bring forth boldness in the messenger; it creates the hope and hunger in the brethren. When we have fiery believers in our midst, we must open our ears and hear the testimony of Jesus. The truth they have encountered transcends human reasoning. Hunger begets hunger. Passion from others can and will awaken our own.

May the love of training up and being trained up return. The Word of the Lord is good for teaching, equipping, correcting, and rebuking, but may it all flow out of authentic relationship. As we are learning more about Jesus's leadership, keep in mind that "a bruised reed he will not break, and a smoldering wick he will not snuff out" (Matt. 12:20 NIV). It is never the job of a leader to snuff out the fire God has placed in His burning ones, if and when stumbling occurs. Instead, let us steward that fire well, stoke it, help cleanse it, and receive from it.

In a hotel room one day, I was pacing back and forth, praying in the Spirit. I had received news that devastated and offended my heart. I had to preach day and night for the next three days. In that moment, I chose to forgive the offense. In my grief, I groaned for the offender to be made clean. Suddenly, a word from the Lord came to me—not concerning my personal situation, but for the worship leader who would be on the platform that evening. *Tell the young man that although he does not really know me yet, I have marked him and chosen him to carry a prophetic sound that will break the chains of compromise off this generation.* Weeping overwhelmed me for this young man, along with thankfulness that the Lord would be willing to call him out of the darkness and into destiny.

That weekend was powerful. The young guy leading worship encountered and was marked by God, but he struggled through his sin for a little longer. The Lord was in hot pursuit of him, and when the timing was right, this fiery one came to a meeting I was holding and has been blazing the earth ever since. This young man became one of my closest spiritual sons. It was years before I realized that out of my pain and choice to forgive an offence that the Lord had birthed a messenger who carried my same DNA. The tenderness of my heart would transform into a fresh anointing. The new anointing would release a word, and fresh wind would blow onto a smoldering wick. The word would transform a prodigal into a true son.

Young ones, I admonish you to listen to those who love you enough to teach you. Not all desire to control or manipulate. Many authentically want to see the earth won for Jesus. The Lord is restoring "the hearts of the fathers to their children and the hearts of the children to their fathers" to bring forth a blessing (Malachi 4:6). In this, all will become mentors to one another. All will be compelled to go! I see the Lord healing the wounded fathers, mothers, and children and great exploits being done hand in hand. I hear the words "permission to go" being trumpeted from heaven into the earth. Beloved, whether you are an established leader or a young firebrand, allow the great *ekballo* to produce a groan, the groan to release a pressing, and the pressing to make way for fresh anointing. The fresh anointing will open the flow of healing and fiery family will be trained up and sent out into the nations.

Permission to Burn

Pray!

Awaken the *ekballo* in my belly. Make me a messenger and a safe place for messengers. I love Your leadership, Jesus. I want to be a sent one, and I want to train, equip, and release. Align me with a mature, holy, lifelong spiritual family. Help me to love deeply and hold lightly those You send into my sphere of influence. Guide me in Your ways. Fashion my heart and character to resemble Yours.

10

THE MARRIAGE OF WISDOM AND ZEAL

As you go, preach, saying, "The kingdom of heaven is at hand." Heal the sick, raise the dead, cleanse the lepers, cast out demons. Freely you received, freely give. Do not acquire gold, or silver, or copper for your money belts. – Matthew 10:7–9

Millennials define faith journeys as a Spartan journey people seek to take by not carrying any money with them on a short mission trip. As they go, they take the Scriptures literally—they fast and pray, seeking the Lord about where to go and trusting Him for a place to stay, food to eat, and money to get around with. They are essentially becoming vagabonds for Jesus.

Permission to Burn

Not long ago, I first heard about something many millennials refer to as a "faith journey," and I found myself deeply concerned. I felt concerned for these zealous fireballs who were going out without wisdom and neglecting their responsibilities. Then I began to realize these young people are not very different from the young, zealous me, who was new to being enamored with Jesus and filled with faith and fire.

Many mature leaders question the validity and sanity of these faith journeys. I do believe we need wisdom along with zeal. These zealous ones need to know they're truly hearing from the Lord before they set out with nothing and disregard the responsibilities at home. Teaching discernment is important. However, as I said in the last chapter, training is essential. If they are honestly following the words of Jesus—even if they incorrectly discern His will on a particular journey—He will be with them to teach them along the way. He loves their faith in Him. I feel strongly in my heart to be a voice of wisdom and guidance but never to discourage anyone from having this kind of incredible faith.

Modern-Day Faith Journeys

It is time for the westernized church to get a little more faith in our culture and in our dreams for Jesus. With all our calculations, loans, revenue, and building projects, we have turned the body of Christ into a business that lacks in faith. We depend more on our pocketbooks than we do on the Lord when it comes to ministry. Don't misunderstand, it's wonderful to have an abundance of surplus finances stored up for the kingdom so we can do all God has called us to do without worry; but we know that's rare for most people, and it does not stretch our faith. In fact, if we feel

The Marriage of Wisdom and Zeal

like we have enough to finance everything God has called us to do, our vision probably is not big enough.

The kingdom of heaven always requires faith, but that does not mean we should become flippant, arrogant, and irresponsible toward our homes, children, jobs, and such to set out with nothing and preach the kingdom. Being full of faith to preach the kingdom is biblical, but neglecting children and family is not. Perhaps the solution to this dilemma is to take the family along, modeling before them a lifestyle of intercession. I cannot explain away Jesus's words, "As you go, preach, saying, 'The kingdom of heaven is at hand.' Heal the sick, raise the dead, cleanse the lepers, cast out demons. Freely you received, freely give. Do not acquire gold, or silver, or copper for your money belts" (Matthew 10:7-9).

Ever since I was young, I have prayed that God would give me wisdom far beyond my years, and I believe He has. I believe it is our responsibility to teach how wisdom and zeal interact when we hear from the Lord. We must know when to go and when to stay. We must know when to fear the Lord enough to trust and obey.

The Bible has much to say about going out, boldly unashamed of the gospel, and it has much to say about wisdom. It's time for the body of Christ to get a surge of revelation concerning the convergence of radical faith and skilful, godly wisdom. When zeal and wisdom marry, the permission and commission to burn, grow, and go will cause a tidal wave of revival. The primary commission of our earthy ministry is found in Matthew 10:7-9 (see above). Sometimes I feel we are very bound by our fear-driven human wisdom, so we don't truly hear the skilful and godly wisdom of the Lord expressed in the Psalms and Proverbs.

Permission to Burn

Godly wisdom is greater than human wisdom. "The fear of the Lord is the beginning of wisdom" (Prov. 9:10). We must have the fear of the Lord to obey His Word in faith; this is the beginning of wisdom. It's not just for the young, zealous new believers to go and preach the message, heal the sick, raise the dead, cleanse the lepers (the diseased ones everyone has given up on), and drive out demons. It is not only for the young ones to take a journey of faith; Jesus gave this commission to the apostles. It is our responsibility to believe God will take care of all the needs of His messengers so we can be part of the solution, not part of the problem. One way we can do this is by giving to those who are going out to do the work of the gospel. Some of us fear the level of thickness of our wallets more than we fear the Lord and His command to go and send. This is the very kingdom-manifesting mission we were saved to accomplish.

Scripture says, "Freely you received, freely give." (Matt. 10:8). We have received a salvation that includes our own healing, deliverance, and freedom from the demons that tormented us before we knew Jesus. Now it is our turn to release what we have received to others. May we all feel deep conviction and fear of the Lord about this so we do not hinder the very essence of the gospel. I pray we are rattled enough to go forth ourselves, with our true ministry, and be among the burning ones ignited by God to bring revival. And if we can't go, may we give in abundance to send.

The Gospel with Power

In His commission, Jesus said signs, wonders, and miracles are just the truth of the gospel being displayed with power. It is our responsibility as leaders to not just impart wisdom

The Marriage of Wisdom and Zeal

to this younger generation, but also to abide in the secret place and live out the gospel ourselves. In doing so, we won't chase after the signs, wonders, and miracles; the signs, wonders and miracles will chase after us. However, the young ones will not see this manifest in truth if we, the mature ones, are not living, breathing examples of the power of God. Mature faith should be greater than the faith of the immature, because the mature have both wisdom and zeal for the Lord. Freely you have received, so freely give. Paul, who was very zealous in preaching the gospel, said, "I am not ashamed of the gospel, for it is the power of God for salvation to everyone who believes" (Rom. 1:16).

I pray we never bring shame to those who proclaim the gospel of Jesus Christ and exemplify the power of God. If we do so, we are not for Him but against Him. When the apostle Paul heard that some were preaching the gospel with bad motives, he said he did not worry about it but celebrated that Christ was being preached. The preaching of the gospel is always a good thing. Let's not stumble over the zeal of those who are purely on fire for Jesus but rather celebrate what God is doing through them. When our hearts are tuned toward gratitude, we will be more open to God's voice and His burning.

The fact is, the gospel has always been a message of supernatural power. If we find ourselves without that power, this should concern us. The apostle Paul wrote, "But realize this, that in the last days difficult times will come. . . . [Men will be] lovers of pleasure rather than lovers of God, holding to a form of godliness, although they have denied its power; avoid such men as these" (2 Timothy 3:1,4-5). We must be careful that we are not walking in a form of godliness while denying its power.

Permission to Burn

This breeds sin of all sorts—hatred, manipulation, sexual immorality, and more. I suggest taking a moment to read the entirety of 2 Timothy 3. This power-lacking form of godliness is a train wreck, and it works against the Lord by trying to shut down those who are walking out the Word of God.

We must always ask ourselves if we are being examples of the true gospel or the ones others are fleeing from. The word "flee" also means to go, so we are to go preach the gospel, and we are also to go away from, or flee, impure religious people who are preventing and perverting the preaching of the powerful gospel.

I experienced this in my life. I was very excited and felt at home with those who were encouraging me to obey the Word of God, which I was consuming day and night. But as soon as people who were speaking into my life began to deny the power of God, I wanted to run. I did not run away from God, but I ran to those who were willing to equip me with a solid foundation in the truth of His Word. I wanted to be close to Him and have that foundation. I wanted to be the best me I could be in Him. This is not rebellion; it is obedience to the Word of the Lord. God has put it in the DNA of those who encounter His Son and are filled with His Spirit, to go, be discipled, and preach the gospel with power.

Live the Lifestyle

The Lord gives us clear direction in His Word, as we see in this passage above from 2 Timothy. Even in life, we often see examples of both the light and the darkness at work. We can see mothers and fathers in the faith who are walking in step with Him and His Word, as well as those who have selfish motives and deny the power of His Word.

The Marriage of Wisdom and Zeal

It is important to look around and find the ones who are proclaiming the truth of the Word of God and living it out. When we look for mentors or leaders, we should look for those who are excited about the truth of the Word of God and have a history of equipping and sending those under their care. Look for the true character of God in their lives. Leaders should be on fire for Jesus and moving in His power rather than lukewarm, arrogant, or condescending about the true move and power of God.

To those who are leaders, I want to encourage you to live the lifestyle of burning for Jesus personally. And I bless you to know how to release those God has brought to you for a season. If you release them well, without holding them captive to your ministry, they will always view you as a father or mother in their lives—someone they can come home to. God does not want us to have broken relationships with people who leave our ministries. Although some relationships will inevitably be broken, we don't take the blame or the glory. Some will join our team for a long season, or even a lifetime, but most will be equipped and sent out.

God wants the local church to be a place these sent ones can call home, even after they go away. This is what it looks like to have a healthy and biblical local church or ministry. The health of our relationships with others is in direct relation to our personal proximity to the Father as sons and daughters. This cycle is similar to that of a healthy family, in which parents release their children to go and live the lives they have trained them to live. They can always come home to visit, but it's never healthy if, after they are sent out, they return home to stay. Healthy parents will encourage their children to remain committed to their new, God-given covenant relationships and destinies, even if they feel more comfortable in their parents' homes.

We must remember this when it comes to ministry. Our job as leaders is to equip, train, and give people permission to obey the Word and voice of God in its fullness. Part of being leaders is embracing the season when God fills our nests with sons and daughters, as well as the season when those sons and daughters get their wings and fly. More children always come.

It is also our job to be examples of those who do what the Father says to do, go when the Father says to go, and release when the Father says to release. Even Jesus said it was better for Him to go away and leave the Helper for His disciples (see John 16:7). Jesus told His disciples they would do greater things than He did (see John 14:12). In the terminology of the world, this means it is our job to work ourselves out of a job. When Jesus was about to ascend back to heaven, He told His disciples, "You will receive power when the Holy Spirit has come upon you; and you shall be My witnesses both in Jerusalem, and in all Judea and Samaria, and even to the remotest part of the earth" (Acts 1:8).

Jesus commissioned the disciples to take over His job on earth. We should do the same. For the purposes of Christ, we are selected and not rejected to expand His work further in the earth for generation after generation. It's time we start preaching the gospel of selection and commission instead of rejection and omission. His commission and purpose for His ascension was to release the power of the Holy Spirit upon His people so they could be true witnesses to His presence in the earth in their hometowns, in regions, and countries, and to the ends of the earth.

The Marriage of Wisdom and Zeal

We Gentiles here in America are the ends of the earth He was talking about when He spoke those words. Because the gospel has reached us, because Jesus has chosen to pour out His Spirit upon generation after generation, those who went before us were released and sent to share the gospel of His dominion with our ancestors. It's our turn in our generation to release and do greater works than He, or even those who went before us, did. We love to quote the "what would Jesus do" saying, but it's time we actually do what Jesus did and continue to do what Jesus is doing. He is giving more than permission; He gave a Great Commission. It is our turn in our generation to keep passing the baton.

Pray!

> I confess this Christ life is a journey of radical faith and heavenly wisdom. You are a master designer. Family was Your idea. Age, gender, race, and skill levels are fibers that make the heavenly system function, but You alone, Holy Spirit, have the power to transform those fibers into an anointed mantel. I call forth the outpouring of You, Spirit, that brings a powerful convergence of the young, old, zealous, and wise. Give me wisdom to know when to hold relationships close and when to let go. Create in me a healthy confidence as your son or daughter. Remove my need to build my own kingdom so I can build Yours. I ask You to use me as You please and align me with others who long to be Your family on fire.

11
Living as Sons and Daughters

This generation of young, fiery harvesters needs its mothers' and fathers' hearts to turn back to it. This is essential for the movement to fully take root in the heart of God. Mothers and fathers and sons and daughters, it's time for us all to grow up and let the mature bride arise.

Permission to Burn

We live in a time of identity confusion. Most of the confusion we are dealing with now, generationally, stems from the patterns of thought developed during the hippie or free-love movement that took place in the '60s and '70s. This movement brought forth a new culture and school of thought that contained confusion masked as counterfeit freedom, as well as counterfeit love and peace. This movement of blatant immorality and bondage gave birth to the massive degeneration of morality that has now disoriented an entire generation.

I believe a generation, biblically, refers to a people who are living upon the earth together. Some say forty to fifty years is a biblical generation. The world's way of measuring a generation is a little different. Sociologists determine generations based on common characteristics or distinctives of a group born within a certain timeframe. For example, most call those born between 1982 and 2000 or so the millennial generation. I am one who has one foot on each side of this generational line, because I was born in January of 1981. Because of this, I can understand the generational rants from both sides.

Honestly, the generational terminology bugs me because I don't think it is how God sees us, but I use it here as a baseline to work from, with the goal of tearing down dividing walls and rebuilding the structure of the body of Christ, so we can fit together to be the house of the living God. So if you are a millennial or younger and you are reading this, hang on and keep burning—I am going somewhere you want to go!

Living as Sons and Daughters

The Millennial Generation Trap Broken

Millennials, who are now emerging leaders in our world, have often been labeled as lazy, immature, and lacking in true social skills, job skills, and commitment. Many also see them as confused concerning the baseline of their identity in most areas of life. They fear leadership yet crave it; they love to be boundless yet long for boundaries. These labels are, in many ways, curses placed upon them by the fathers and mothers who gave them life. We forget it was the mothers and fathers who pioneered these ideologies and gave birth to this so-called technologically crippled, dependent, and lazy generation.

Sadly, the schools of thought birthed in the '60s and '70s now have infiltrated our families, churches, and spiritual leadership as truth. This is similar to the hellenization of the Jewish people, which caused God's chosen people to turn to idolatry and the associated Hebrew schools of thought, and to eventually adopt the Greek system—a largely endorsed polytheistic compromise and the adoption of foreign gods.

For Americans and those in Western cultures, our form of polytheism—the worship and acceptance of multiple gods—is humanism. According to the *Merriam-Webster Dictionary*, humanism is "an outlook or system of thought attaching prime importance to human rather than divine or supernatural matters." Any time a culture accepts a system of human thought and refuses to fight for the living power and holy purity of the one true God, a slippery slope of godless, powerless generational sowing and reaping occurs.

The Bible tells us the parents' sins influence generations to come. In Deuteronomy 5:9, it says the sins of the father are visited upon the children to the third and fourth generation. This is sobering to think about. A dad can influence generations to come with his sin and unbelief. This is not a mystical curse placed upon people by God because of their parents' deeds. It is a system of sowing and reaping from one generation to the next. When belief systems of immorality are mingled with spiritual belief systems or fear-based religion, it creates a process of spiritual sowing and reaping into the next generation. This sets the stage for a wayward and rebellious lifestyle that falsely declares that any lifestyle is acceptable to God.

But when people stand against belief systems they know do not align with scriptural truth and are willing to give their lives to destroy the false, while also being empowered by the Spirit to bring conviction of truth in love, that truth rushes in to shift the next generation into radical spiritual sonship in identity, truth, and freedom. The curse can be broken in one generation. All it takes is a bold flame of holy fire to believe and declare "Not I, but Christ in me!" and change the course of history. This bold voice fathers a generation of bold, uncompromising messengers who may not know the great impact of their lives as reformers until they meet Jesus face-to-face.

On the cross, Jesus broke the curse once and for all, and He commissioned us to enforce this by bringing His kingdom family revelation "on earth as it is in heaven" (Matt. 6:10). This is our hope. When we look at the issues, we see swarming around us in the light of the cross, we see the truth of what is possible. Every generation has received the blessing of God our Father to be sons and daughters, not slaves to the seeds sown by the mistakes of the previous generation. In truth, the effects of a godly father or mother who is willing to break the curse will outlast the effects of an unbelieving father or mother who sets the curse in motion.

ALWAYS HOPE

King Josiah, in his generation, changed the course of history by discovering the truth about God's disgust for idolatry. When he discovered the book of the law, he wept and tore his clothes. He delivered the people from the bondage of a curse by destroying the abominable idolatry his forefathers had instituted and passively allowed. Josiah discovered the truth and acted on it with a deep conviction that brought cleansing, awakening, and freedom in his generation. Josiah did "what was right in the sight of the Lord and followed completely the ways of his father David, not turning aside to the right or the left" (2 Kings 22:2 NIV).

Although the king who succeeded Josiah muddled things up again, we still read Josiah's story and use his boldness to inspire us in our own fight to destroy the idolatry of our generation. Josiah is known as a son of David rather than associated with his evil father, Amon. The truth is, Josiah's decision to weep, pray, and act is still reaping fruit in our lives.

Much teaching about sowing and reaping, cursing and blessing, came from the Charismatic Movement of the '80s and '90s, but that movement did not teach much on bringing our Father's family into the freedom of spiritual identity. The primary focus was on spiritual correction. Teachers like Jack Frost and Jack Hayford were voices crying out in the wilderness. They included teaching on inner healing and deliverance from generational curses, and they also wove in the affirmation and blessing of the love of God as the Father. I, personally, was radically impacted by the ministry of Jack Frost in my first few years of healing from the trauma of sexual abuse.

Unfortunately, teachings and attitudes of cursing and condemnation toward millennials are often heard the loudest because of the rise of social media. Instead, we should be teaching authentic, tough-love mentorship, renewal, and blessing. Negative teachings do more harm than good. We need true, holy, and bold fathers and mothers to arise—those who personally know the love of the Father for themselves and are, therefore, able to lead others into an understanding of their identity in the Father.

Tear Down and Build Up

We are not just called to tear things down but also to resurrect and rebuild. Jesus, in His zeal for His Father's house to be a house of prayer, turned over the tables of the corrupt money changers in the temple. He hated the way they took advantage of the people's desire to obey God and sacrifice to Him. When the people demanded that He prove His authority to do such a thing, He answered with an odd statement: "Destroy this temple, and in three days I will raise it up" (John 2:19). He knew the only way to tear down the man-made system of worship was to give up His own life for the very leaders He was angry with.

The temple leaders thought Jesus was threatening to tear down the physical temple, but Jesus meant the system would be destroyed, and a new system of worship would be reborn from His death and resurrection. Jesus wasn't nearly as concerned with their building as they thought. He was a lot more concerned for them to know the freedom found in living beyond the veil of separation and the altar of animal sacrifice. Jesus would rebuild what He would tear down with His own blood. Jesus's correction was not to harm the leaders at all but to bring awakening to every person in the temple that day. He was about to bless them with a new, beautiful, living structure of day-and-night worship that can't be bought or sold.

We have been positioned like King Josiah to bring freedom from idolatry to our generation. We have also been positioned, like Jesus, to rebuild a people who will be the living day-and-night temple of the presence of God. For this reason, we must repent of and deny the labels of our culture about both millennials and their parents. In our God-given DNA, we carry the ability to shake the foundations of everything that exalts itself above the knowledge of God. We were born for such a time as this.

Millennials need the fathers and mothers to repent of the bashing and to be willing to teach them wisdom in the fear and admonition of the Lord. But at the same time, these mentors would benefit greatly from hearing of the beauty, awe, and wonder of the Father's love that these millennials are clinging to so tightly. We need wisdom, zeal, love, and correction now more than ever. We are not to excuse the areas that they may misuse, such as grace and lack of holiness. We are to tear down and build up.

Hear the heart cry of the Father to awaken us all to sonship. There is a deeper place of our identity that He longs to take us into as the ruling bride of Christ. This Father's love revelation is being poured out over us all, sovereignly, to heal issues of identity confusion. Hand in hand, we are living on this earth together, in this moment, to give birth to and to raise up one of the greatest moves of God the world has ever seen. *Together* is the key. Factions and divisions are lies of the enemy. "[He has] raised us up together, and made us sit together in the heavenly places in

Permission to Burn

Christ Jesus" (Ephesians 2:6 NKJV). The heavenly places in Christ do not have a section for youth and college students and a separate section for the adults. We are all in this together.

The Birth of a Bridal Awakening

At the same time as the hippie or free-love movement was growing, a countercultural revolution called the Jesus People movement also arose. It caught much traction and transformed masses of young people to live in the freedom of the true love and true peace of Jesus. God wants to do a similar thing in our day. Although the enemy has sown many tares among the wheat in our modern church culture, I believe it is harvest time. Now we will begin to see the wheat and the tares separate.

The exposure of false ideologies and thought systems is on the rise. Many counterfeits exist, some of which look very much like the real thing. False mysticism and certain false teachings promote rebellion as counterfeit freedom. They offer counterfeit love, counterfeit peace, counterfeit miracles, and so forth. These are the tares. Fortunately, they are being exposed now and will become more evident in the near future.

The Bible tells us cleansing always comes first to the household of God before the rest of the world (see 1 Pet. 4:17). Jesus's parable of the wheat and the tares explains this in greater detail and helps us see what is taking place prophetically in our church culture. The parable goes like this:

> The kingdom of heaven may be compared to a man who sowed good seed in his field. But while his men were sleeping, his enemy came and sowed

tares among the wheat, and went away. But when the wheat sprouted and bore grain, then the tares became evident also. The slaves of the landowner came and said to him, "Sir, did you not sow good seed in your field? How then does it have tares?" And he said to them, "An enemy has done this!"

The slaves said to him, "Do you want us, then, to go and gather them up?" But he said, "No; for while you are gathering up the tares, you may uproot the wheat with them. Allow both to grow together until the harvest; and in the time of the harvest I will say to the reapers, 'First gather up the tares and bind them in bundles to burn them up; but gather the wheat into my barn.'"

- Matthew 13:24-30

A tare is more than just a weed, it is a species of ryegrass in which the seeds are strong, soporific poison. It resembles wheat until the ear appears; only then can the difference be discovered. Tares grow plentifully in Syria and Palestine. They have also been known to attach themselves to the root system of the wheat rather than grow from their own source—the tares try to use the actual wheat as a host. A tare is difficult to identify because it counterfeits the real, but it eventually shows its true identity when the fruit buds. Because of this, it cannot be removed until the entire field is harvested. Trying to remove a tare before harvest endangers the root system of the true wheat. When harvest time comes, the tares reveal themselves and are easily identified. The farmer need not go through excess work to remove the tares before the harvest. He will know the tare by its fruit, and at the time of harvest, he can remove it and throw it into the fire to be destroyed, seed and all. This is very powerful and freeing when we think about Jesus's statement about fruit.

> You will know them by their fruits. Grapes are not gathered from thorn bushes nor figs from thistles, are they? So every good tree bears good fruit, but the bad tree bears bad fruit. A good tree cannot produce bad fruit, nor can a bad tree produce good fruit. Every tree that does not bear good fruit is cut down and thrown into the fire. So then, you will know them by their fruits.
>
> – Matthew 7:16-20

I believe we are in an hour of the truth being revealed and the false being exposed. Over the past twenty years or so, the prayer movement has set the stage for the Lord to give increase to the spiritual seeds that have been planted and watered with nonstop intercession. Healthy harvesters have been learning how to tend the heavenly fields as a lifestyle, instead of using carnal tools to frantically pluck out what may be a tare and destroying the healthy growing wheat. They have learned how to trust in the Lord to remove the imposters when harvest time comes, seed and all. Meanwhile, they contend in joyful intercession and enjoy seeing the field grow up during the season of waiting.

The Lord is now saying the harvest of souls is ready. All the while, we have seen indicators and warning signs, but the Lord of the harvest is sending forth laborers into the field, and they are on fire. They will bring in the sheaths of harvest, and the fire they carry will expose and remove the tares. Many dreams, visions, and words from the Lord have been quickening our spiritual discernment to see the counterfeit, even when the culture around us is trying to force us to accept or tolerate what we know is false.

Living as Sons and Daughters

As the hearts of the fathers and mothers are turned back to the sons and daughters, and the sons and daughters to the fathers and mothers, we will begin to see a maturity arise that crosses generational lines. We will see a true kingdom movement of honor, humility, purity, and freedom. This movement will be accompanied by Jesus stretching forth His hand to do signs, wonders, and miracles through these unapologetically pure and holy, love-ravished harvesters of fire; but the credit will be His alone, and the Father will be glorified like never before. Many are calling this massive harvest of souls, which will be accompanied by signs, wonders, and miracles, the explosion of a new Jesus movement, but I prophesy right now that this Jesus movement will quickly turn into the sound of the love-sick cry of the mature bride of Christ, awakening all over the earth.

Engrained in this generation is a spiritual awareness unlike that of any generation before. This generation has a discernment sovereignly given by God to usher in an unprecedented movement. Gifts and talents will explode in the arts to express the spiritual awakening and creativity of the Father. He has gifted these emerging leaders to sing, paint, and play in majestic ways, and to preach with boldness according to the blueprint of heaven. However, along with the awakening of the spiritual senses in this generation, the counterfeit mystical movement and humanistic spirit of compromise has also made its way into our Christian circles.

Sexual perversion and identity confusion have made it difficult for this generation to get a hold on what is real and what is false. These are the tares that are now being forced to reveal their fruit. The free-love movement or hippie movement of our generation has despised correction and embraced lingo counterfeiting love as tolerance. Tolerance of sin has been called love when in fact it is the opposite. It has infiltrated Christendom and is widely accepted in the church. That is why this generation of young, fiery harvesters needs its mothers' and fathers' hearts to turn back to it. This is essential for the movement to fully take root in the heart of God.

Our maturity has been greatly lacking, and our discernment is watered down because of a deficiency of rich scriptural teaching and real biblical love. Our receptivity to loving correction is very low, because out of the same mouth have come blessing and cursing. Mothers and fathers and sons and daughters, it's time for us all to grow up and let the mature bride arise.

> Though by this time you ought to be teachers, you have need again for someone to teach you the elementary principles of the oracles of God, and you have come to need milk and not solid food. For everyone who partakes only of milk is not accustomed to the word of righteousness, for he is an infant. But solid food is for the mature, who because of practice have their senses trained to discern good and evil.
>
> – Hebrews 5:12-14

The longer we allow ourselves to stay inside a system that embraces the world's nature, the more we are like sheep without shepherds, becoming needy and lukewarm. We were created to consume the meat of the Word at a very young age. Many of us were filled with Holy Spirit even in the womb. But those with wings have been bound and unable to fly. They have returned to milk because many of the leaders who have been feeding them cannot consume solid food themselves. Many of these so-called fathers and mothers are identifying the orphaned heart in this generation, but they are perpetuating the problem by building their own kingdoms.

Abandonment and rejection will not be healed by merely pointing this generation to a man or a woman who calls himself or herself a spiritual parent. A human cannot fill that need or give that identity of sonship. We can be friends, mentors, disciples, and teachers as sons or daughters ourselves. Only the heavenly Father can heal broken, rejected, immature, and orphaned hearts. Many lack biological and spiritual fathers and mothers, and they do need human spiritual parents; however, much of the spiritual fathering movement has become self-serving. This movement identifies the orphan heart and calls it out, only to bind the gifted-yet-needy orphan into a system of spiritual slavery. We need the pure and mature bride to arise.

In many ways, this unhealth has happened to build human mega-ministry kingdoms. Sadly, many of these so-called fathers and mothers have become gods unto themselves. They do not give sons and daughters permission to go, burn, or do anything else unless it benefits them. Many have fostered this unknowingly out of a deep need for personal identity. Others have knowingly created networks that lead abandoned and rejected young ministers into dependency on humanistic spiritual adoption. They use endearing terms like sons and fathers, but beneath the surface lurks a slavery mentality. The use of biblical lingo with needy, wounded hearts causes entrapment, which serves the "father's" vision but disregards the needs of the children.

Permission to Burn

As a young minister, I experienced the "serve your way up" terminology, which is used to entice people to earn a position and platform. However, a platform gained this way often becomes a place of prostitution of the gifts. It is used to earn love and value in the kingdom of the ministry god and the false father. The moment people realize that spiritual prostitution is happening, leaders of this counterfeit kingdom create a deep fear in its followers of spiritual rebellion and cursing in the mind and heart. My hope is that this system is being exposed and the true fathering heart is arising. This is essential, because fathering or mothering is an important part of earthly discipleship, and we have to get beyond the orphan-hearted teachings and into the eternal identity that we are to be one wholly mature bride.

In the coming new Jesus movement, the sons' hearts are returning to the fathers and the fathers' hearts to the sons. The playing field is being leveled, and the false hierarchy is crumbling. Old and young alike are being healed and coming into identity as sons and daughters of God, not sons and daughters of the man-made ministry gods. The true Father is bringing down the false unity movement, much like the Tower of Babel. He is releasing a real kingdom movement like the outpouring of His Spirit did (in Acts 2)—when His followers stood in the hidden place in one accord. A new, heavenly language is being released, like the tongues of fire, and the old is being scattered and confused.

The wheat and the tares will be harvested and separated. A remnant that is large in this generation is arising. They know who they are, because they know who their Dad is. Spiritual mothers and fathers will learn to be humble and to become sons and daughters themselves.

LIVING AS SONS AND DAUGHTERS

True family in the kingdom is being awakened again. False mentorship and discipleship connections are being exposed for what they are—schemes to grow human kingdoms rather than God's. The real ministry of making disciples (not slaves) will arise and shine. The fivefold ministry gifts will be reidentified as gifts given only by the grace of God, designed to glorify Him. No longer will God our Father allow our gifts to be our identity. Our identity will be in Him, and eventually we will begin to understand that we are the bride of His Son. Then the precious gift of kingdom dominion will flow freely, giving all the glory to the Son and Bridegroom, Jesus Christ.

A new thing is taking shape. No eye has seen and no ear has heard, nor has it entered the hearts of people, what God has in store for those who love Him (see 1 Cor. 2:9). The unexpected is to be expected, because dreams are going to become reality.

We have permission to dream!

Let's go beyond praying for ourselves.

BEGIN TO INTERCEDE

> Father, awaken the dream of heaven inside us. Destroy the false and reveal the truth in the fields. Teach us to be a praying church so that when You swing the sickle of harvest, we aren't offended but ready to gather. Prepare Your people for the revealing and removal of the tares. Bring forth the mature sons and daughters. Awaken the bride and make us ready for the great harvest.

12
Dreaming Heaven's Dreams

At once I was in the Spirit, and there before me was a throne in heaven with someone sitting on it. And the one who sat there had the appearance of jasper and ruby. A rainbow that shone like an emerald encircled the throne. Surrounding the throne were twenty-four other thrones, and seated on them were twenty-four elders. They were dressed in white and had crowns of gold on their heads. From the throne came flashes of lightning, rumblings and peals of thunder. In front of the throne, seven lamps were blazing. These are the seven spirits of God. – Revelation 4:2–5 NIV

Constant and consistent worship, prayer, awe, wonder, lightnings, flashings, fire, and glory happen around the throne of God. God our Father, the Creator of the universe, is always dreaming and creating. He never stops. All creatures who set their eyes on Him are overwhelmed by His beauty. Incredibly, He invites us into that wonder and amazement very single day. He calls us higher to see and hear what He sees and hears. This is what the apostle John experienced on Patmos.

When we water the gospel message down to a mere check in a religious box, we barely tap into the amazement of the relationship Jesus gave His life for so we might truly live. Enough of mediocrity. Jesus dares us to dream the dreams of heaven. He says, "You are not *just* worth dying for. Now I invite you to live for Me, to dream with Me, to see what I see and call it forth into the earth with Me." Jesus is seated at the right hand of the Father, and the angelic host of heaven is gazing upon His beauty.

And to you and me, He gives permission to be part of bringing this heavenly reality into the earth. He tells us to pray to our Father in heaven, "Your kingdom come. Your will be done, on earth as it is in heaven" (Matt. 6:10). He says, "Come up here, sit with me, and I'll show you what I see so you can pray for it to be made manifest where you live" (see Eph. 2:6; Rev. 4:1; 11:12; paraphrase mine).

Jesus lives, and He gave us His Spirit as our Helper so we can see what He sees. He has created us not just to be born again of the Spirit as a theological doctrine, but to experience the reality of that doctrine by living as spiritual beings. This is the true life that comes from the new birth Jesus taught Nicodemus about (in John 2–3).

Dreaming Heaven's Dream

John was given his vision of the throne room (in Revelation 4) not just to release a prophecy of the second coming of the Lord Jesus, but also so he could see what worship looks like in heaven. This vision helped him to dream God-sized dreams, to pray like Jesus taught him to pray, and to call forth into the earth the depth of love-sick worship, awe, and wonder He saw around the throne. Jesus was daring John, His beloved friend, to dream with Him for a beautiful, spotless, worshipping bride and to see what He sees. As Paul said, "Things which eye has not seen and ear has not heard, and which have not entered the heart of man, all that God has prepared for those who love Him" (1 Cor. 2:9). John was the disciple Jesus loved (see John 19:26), and he had a vision that enabled him to dream heaven's dreams.

King David, the man after God's own heart, was another dreamer (see Acts 13:22). David, who also longed to build on earth what he had seen in heaven, caught a glimpse of the desire of God to dwell with humanity. David longed to dwell in the house of the Lord forever, not just to hang out in a building but "that I may dwell in the house of the Lord all the days of my life, to behold the beauty of the Lord" (Ps. 27:4). David saw something he could never unsee. He was gripped by the image of relational, nonstop worship, intercession, and encounters with the Lord.

The prophet Isaiah was also a dreamer. His encounter (in Isaiah 6) led him from a place of fear, trembling, and weakness to a place of boldness: "Woe is me, for I am undone! Because I am a man of unclean lips, and I dwell in the midst of a people of unclean lips," (Isa. 6:5 NKJV) to "Here am I. Send me!" (v. 8). Isaiah was undone, cleansed, and ruined by his vision of the holy one.

Permission to Burn

In this way, the dreams of heaven became the dreams of mere men. Their encounters made them into laid-down lovers. These lovers would rather die than give up the dreams of heaven that burned in their souls. More than kingdom sons, they were love-sick lovers who no longer identified themselves with the pattern of this world.

God's Dream Was You

God is a dreamer, but He does not end at the dream. He accomplishes what He sends forth His word to do. "So will My word be which goes forth from My mouth; it will not return to Me empty without accomplishing what I desire, and without succeeding in the matter for which I sent it" (Isaiah 55:11).

God's dream was you. The Father didn't crush His Son just so you could go to heaven. Our relationship with the Son, and the privilege of sharing in His inheritance, is actually the greatest reward. The sky is the limit in Him. We are His joy and reward. Paul called Jesus the second Adam who didn't fall into sin like the first (see 1 Corinthians 15:45). We are the second bride who will reign with Him forever. His bride gets to have His wild, earth-changing dreams and desires in her heart as she lays down her tiny, feeble, fleshly desires and takes up His. As we begin to seek His face, our faces shine, hope arises, and we begin to dream crazy, God-sized dreams. These dreams come from His heart, and because of that, we can be confident they will come to pass. They are supposed to be bigger than us.

I am not saying every dream is a God dream. It is not. What I am saying is that when the dream is found in the Scriptures and birthed in our hearts from the secret place of prayer, it is found in Him, and we'd better believe He

Dreaming Heaven's Dream

will accomplish it. He is inviting us to dream with Him. That is why every permission He grants begins and ends with us longing for Him. "Seek first His kingdom and His righteousness, and all these things will be added to you" (Matt. 6:33).

God's dreams are always bigger than ours. Consider what He showed John (in Revelation 4). At that point, John's biggest dream was likely just to meet with Jesus on that lonely island where he had been exiled. He had no idea he would see, hear, and write the most mysterious prophecy ever recorded. He could not even conceive of the dream he was about to encounter. And what about Mary, the mother of Jesus? She would never have thought to dream of being the mother of the awaited Messiah. These dreams were so much bigger than the people who bore them in their hearts.

Jesus promised us the pure in heart will see God (see Matt. 5:8). Let's dream of seeing Him and encountering His love. Let's dream of knowing Him and His ways as Moses did. When we do, we will find ourselves dreaming of things much bigger than our humanity. As we long for the Creator, we will find that our wildest dreams were never wild enough. As we come to know who we are in Him, we will see that because we are His bride, His longing is to say, "Yes! Permission granted! Come up here and I'll show you things not yet seen, so I can awaken your heart to Mine and give you the desires I created you to accomplish—as your mandate, both in heaven and on earth."

God is such a good Father! The way He includes us in His dreams is so beautiful. Instead of just accomplishing His dreams on His own, He creates people like us and awakens in us the desire to dream His dreams. He invites us to be bearers of His presence and experience love so

Permission to Burn

deep that we can't help but dream of building Him a place to dwell with us, like David, or of being the place where He dwells, like Mary, or of knowing His beauty and being His bride—like me.

Cry Out!

> Awaken the dream of heaven within me and my family. Encounter me with Your beauty and Your presence. Encounter my family, my church, my workplace. I want to be a bearer of Your presence. This is why I am alive.

13
BIRTHING THE BRIDE

In the same way that the bridegroom, Jesus, was born from the womb of a woman, so will it be with the awakening of His love-sick bride in these last days! The first birth was the physical birth of Jesus into the world, but the second is a spiritual emergence of the global bridal identity.

Permission to Burn

Soon after I married, I found myself pondering why people around me were not happy in ministry or church. Even a well-known pastor told me not to go into ministry, because he said ministry would kill my fire. He said it would be better to go into the workplace. What I didn't know was that ministry had hurt him and his marriage was in a mess, and he gave me this advice from that place of woundedness. I didn't understand. To me, in my raw innocence, it seemed like ministry had to be *the life*. It was the place where I could burn for Jesus all the time. I could pray, study the Word, love on people, and share Him with people every day, all day, for the rest of my life. That's all I wanted to do.

At the time I was freshly out of Bible college, getting ready to get my license and ordination, yet I was having this confusing conversation with a megachurch pastor—one I literally thought walked on water. He pastored a burning, fiery church, yet somehow he seemed to not be happy with being a pastor. Instead, he told me to not go into ministry and get a normal job somewhere. I couldn't understand it. It seemed either he didn't believe in me, or he was just trying to keep me from going through something he had been through.

Permission to Speak

Fast forward seventeen years, and I understand the wounding that can happen as a warrior in ministry. Through my season of coming head to head with the silencing spirit of legalism, I continued to hear the voice of God, and my encounters with Him increased in intensity. In my times of coming to Him with the pain of rejection and the fire in my bones, He always reminded me of how much He loved me, how much He loved those who had hurt me, and how He had called and chosen me. He would show me, and burn into my heart, His desire to bring awakening and revival to my generation. I saw many ministers publicly fall into moral failure and sin. My cry was, "Lord, keep me humble and pure. Don't ever allow me to stand on a platform that will cause me to fall into sin against you."

I didn't fully understand these terms, or the threshing I would go through to stay humble and pure, but I did understand how badly the world needed to encounter God's love and holiness and not just hear another sermon preached on it. He began to give me dreams and desires to gather friends and family around His presence, so we could all learn how to be awakened to more of Him and to sustain true revival in this place of encounter. Often I would think of the times when I went to the church that had the forty days of prayer and fasting, and how that had the potential to really birth His dream for His church. I wondered, *What if we didn't stop at forty days but just lived as a church in His presence?* The dreamer in me would take off then and begin to think of the whole earth living like this, and how it would bring real lifestyle revival to the earth. Then I would tell people about it. At that time, I didn't know about the International House of Prayer in Kansas City, Missouri, or Lou Engle, who was filling stadiums with people my age whose hearts also burned with the same desires. Sometimes it felt like I was talking to the walls.

When the spirit of prophecy rose up in me, I would speak His word and talk like a love-sick fool. This seemed to annoy people greatly. Some even took my passion as rebellion. I wept often, because I felt like I was bound in my own fire. I didn't know this fire would grow into more, the closer I got to Him. Acceptance and being heard and understood by people would never satisfy me anyway. I would think back to the advice of the megachurch pastor and come to know more what he and his wife must have been enduring. I would pray for him to be restored to his first love. I would pray for my heart to not be hardened.

As I endured personal sifting and silencing, I asked God to make me love what He loves and hate what He hates. I asked for the supernatural strength to forgive, heal quickly, and move on from attacks and rejection. He took me into a long season of feeling what He felt over issues of injustice for the innocent. I could feel the way these issues grieved His heart. I wanted so badly to be His hands and feet, and He directed a lot of that passion into fasting and intercession toward social justice issues like abortion, modern-day slavery, and sex trafficking. Our church was very active in praying to end abortion and ministering to girls in crisis situations. I am very thankful for their stance on these issues and how they answered the call to pray and be active in loving the victims and the offenders. Given what the Lord had delivered me out of, these issues hit home for me.

In all this, I had no idea I was racing toward a life-changing moment. Soon I would be slammed with a revelation of His beauty in a stadium gathering, and an invitation from the Lord to trumpet a message He would be branding on my heart. The passion that got me to that stadium was only a drop in the bucket compared to the passion I carried with me when I left. It started when I received a forwarded email from a man named Lou Engle in 2007. I received that email as a word from the Lord, and I answered the call. Below is a portion of that email that specifically spoke to my heart. In it, Lou Engle talked about how corporate repenting as a nation, coupled with fasting and praying about abortion and the perverted sexualization of our nation, would cause God to pour out His Spirit and heal our land. This is the call I answered.

> What must we do? God's holy prescription for our diseased state in times of national crisis and moral collapse is a solemn assembly of united fasting and prayer.
>
> "Now, therefore," says the Lord, "Turn to Me with all your heart, with fasting, with weeping, and with mourning." So rend your heart, and not your garments; return to the Lord your God, for He is gracious and merciful, slow to anger, and of great kindness; and He relents from doing harm."
> - Joel 2:12-13 NKJV
>
> Blow the trumpet in Zion, consecrate a fast, call a sacred assembly; gather the people, sanctify the congregation, assemble the elders, gather the children and nursing babes; let the bridegroom go out from His chamber, and the bride from her dressing room.
> - vv. 15-16 NKJV
>
> Then the Lord will be zealous for His land. . . . "And it shall come to pass afterward that I will pour out My Spirit on all flesh; your sons and your daughters shall prophesy, your old men shall dream dreams, your young men shall see visions.
> - vv. 18, 28 NKJV

I attended this meeting in Nashville, Tennessee, where 70,000 young people joined together in fasting and prayer. I went with my family and some of the remnant people from our church who were very passionate about ending abortion and seeing revival. I fasted for the entire forty days leading up to the event. When I got there, I lay on my stomach in one-hundred-degree heat in that stadium, overwhelmed again by the power and presence of God.

Suddenly, a few hours into the twelve-hour gathering, I was taken up into an encounter with Jesus. I saw Him as the Bridegroom and myself as the bride. It was as though the Lord was delivering on His promise in Joel 2:16, but in a more real way than I'd ever expected. "Let the bridegroom come out of his room and the bride out of her bridal chamber." He was coming out of His chamber to meet His bride. I could see Him in all His glory, high and lifted up. The clouds literally looked as though they parted so I could watch and somehow participate with this grand heavenly scene. I saw a procession of His bride coming to Him, as described in Revelation.

> Then I heard what sounded like a great multitude, like the roar of rushing waters and like loud peals of thunder, shouting: "Hallelujah! For our Lord God Almighty reigns. Let us rejoice and be glad and give him glory! For the wedding of the Lamb has come, and his bride has made herself ready. Fine linen, bright and clean, was given her to wear." (Fine linen stands for the righteous acts of God's holy people.) Then the angel said to me, "Write this: Blessed are those who are invited to the wedding supper of the Lamb!" And he added, "These are the true words of God."
>
> – Revelation 19:6-9 NIV

I heard the shouts and the celebrations. I heard the sound of worship and praise as the bride joined her

BIRTHING THE BRIDE

Bridegroom. I could hear and see this crazy celebration that all of heaven had been yearning for. I could hear the Spirit say come, and the matching cry of the bride crying out come, as in Revelation 22:17. The Lord was high and lifted up, and the train of His robe filled the space above the entire stadium. He was exceedingly happy and full of longing for His bride. For four hours, I was so caught up in this encounter, so completely overwhelmed by the beauty and power of His presence, that I didn't realize I was still on earth.

After that experience at The Call in 2007, I threw off every binder and shackle that man-made theology had attempted to box me into. My heart was flooded with radical love, and I decided to burn for Jesus every day of my life. He is my Groom, their Groom, our Groom! What I saw was a vision of things to come—one day He will return and take His bride up with Him, as He has promised. From that point on, I knew I would never be satisfied unless every day, for the rest of my life, I pursued that one thing David talked about—to dwell in His temple and gaze on His beauty day and night, forever and ever. I was completely encapsulated in love, and the wonderful fear of the Lord gripped my heart.

In that encounter, God also seared my life with a fiery branding. Consecration, holiness, and hunger for Him alone would be my lifelong, love-sick pursuit. This would be my message. I heard His words, *Permission to burn, to speak, to go, and to live in the love-sick bridal revelation!* I heard those words echoing though my innermost being but simultaneously echoing throughout all time. He said to me, *I am giving you a message that you will release to the nations, and that message is first love longing. You will awaken My bride and birth a holy, love-sick bridal movement in the earth that will impact generations to come.* I saw that the fivefold ministry would arise in purity from the place of pure, Spirit-led worship, preaching, and intercession.

This movement will be about lifting up the Bridegroom, Jesus. The conception and birth of many dreams will take place in the lives of His people as they return to their first love. I have seen and heard, and I will never be the same again. Only out of the place of bridal identity can the church, His called-out ones, reign with the Bridegroom. Only from that place can righteous justice be served. We can't get caught up in the terminology; we simply need to understand the longings of our Father. His longing is to give us back the kingdom of heaven and dominion on the earth, as well as the daily heavenly communion and pleasure of the garden of Eden.

The intimacy that birthed humanity began in a garden (in Genesis 1), and sin found its way into that same garden far too quickly (by Genesis 3). It was also in a garden that Jesus gave His life first in His prayer of surrender—in the garden of Gethsemane (see Matt. 26:36). In intercession, before He went to the cross, He committed His life to reversing the curse of sin. He did this when He said, "My Father, if it is possible, let this cup pass from Me; yet not as I will, but as You will" (Matt. 26:39). Jesus was on a mission to win back His bride in that garden. He also rose again in a garden.

It was no accident that Jesus first locked eyes with and spoke the name of the desperate, broken, love-sick Mary in a garden, or that she thought Him the gardener (see John 20:1-18). The garden is the place of encounter. It's the place where the vine grows and is pure. It's the place of reproduction and blissful encounter that leads us to release the kingdom of heaven's government into the earth. It's

Birthing the Bride

the place where He births new things and creates pure dreams. Let's do kingdom dominion, reigning, warring, occupying, and all the activities of the Scriptures. But first, let's experience the eternal pleasure of communion with our Bridegroom. In this place, all God's other things are conceived.

The Bride and Her Beloved

> [The Bridegroom-King:] I have come to you, my darling bride, for you are my paradise garden.
> - Song of Solomon 4:15 TPT

> [The Groom:] I have come into my garden, my sister, my bride.
> - Song of Solomon 5:1 NIV

Many people's hearts have begun to stir to blow the trumpet concerning the mysteries of heaven spoken in secret to pure hearts all over the world. I see a company of pure-hearted and humble lovers arising in the earth—people who know who they are because they know who their God is. His residue is all over them. They have been with Him, and it is evident. They have learned to first blow the trumpet in heaven around the throne of God in prayer before ever speaking of the things they hear and see on the earth. They know to "come boldly to the throne of grace" and to live "seated . . . with Him in heavenly places" (Heb. 4:16 NKJV; Eph. 2:6).

This is not where their journeys began, but it is where they have found the reason for their lives. Many of these lovers once thought they wanted platforms, prestige, and popularity, until they tasted of the goodness of God's presence in the secret place. Then these messengers of heaven realized these platform experiences were sweet only for a moment but could never satisfy the soul. They know they were created for greatness, and they have been through the process of purification, a process we all must yield our lives to. Now they're longing to trumpet the message of heaven with their beloved Bridegroom, not of their own accord.

Rejection no longer manifests bitterness in them. They know rejection does not exist in the throne room of heaven, where they run to and abide. They long to do what they see Him do and say what they hear Him say. In His timing and with the tone of His voice, they only want to release His heart. They have endured persecution, but these trials have taught them how to minister to God before they minister to people. This is now where they feel the most alive. They have rejected the world's counterfeits for greatness and taken up their Father's hidden business of changing the world from His secret place. Greatness is bowing low and lifting Him on high.

Paul said we are seated with Jesus, our great intercessor (see Ephesians 2). We can learn a lot from sitting in that place and working the way Jesus works. From this heavenly place, we execute His longings and prayers into the earth. This is the place where many of these hidden ones have found themselves awakened to the greatness of knowing Him and being known by Him.

Ending Identity Confusion

So much identity confusion exists in our nation and culture. I believe it is a direct result of mass confusion concerning those who call themselves sons and daughters of God, yet are not. Secular humanism has married itself to religion in many ways and created a Goliath of a stronghold. However, the beautiful thing happening is that, in the time of pressing, many have found who they are in Christ. It is amazing how many are coming to know the power of living a lifestyle of purity and love-sick prayer and fasting, not legalism, because of the emergence of true messengers of God. These true messengers aren't just in pulpits or speaking in conferences; they are following the leading of the Lord and going to the streets, college campuses, and coffee shops around America, plucking a generation out of confusion. The big ol' impure, humanistic Goliath is being destroyed by little worshiping Davids who have been trained in the throne room's wilderness places.

It's time to let the humble, pure, and hidden take the microphones to share what they are seeing around the throne of God and in the harvest fields. As the body of Christ, we must begin to give more than human permission. We must also give a commission to those who may not seem outwardly qualified to speak, but who have a message from God burning in their hearts. "Man looks at the outward appearance, but the Lord looks at the heart" (1 Sam. 16:7).

For whatever reason, when the fire first began to burn in me, leaders around me didn't understand the burning and questioned my validity. Maybe it was my gender, my age, or my background; or maybe it was because my delivery was quite zealous and accompanied by tears and a lot of roaring prayer, which was far from a three-point sermon. Earthly leaders silenced me for a long, hard season, but it worked out for the glory of God. The sad truth is this: the religious have been silencing God's unlikely voices in the church for hundreds of years, including the less-astute voices of women, children, and people of color. It's important for us to recognize this so we see that some of the man-made religious traditions have played a part in the identity confusion in the world and in the church. Jesus and His church are the answer, but we have not done the greatest job being that answer. Many people groups have grown angry because they were not recognized as being legitimate in Christendom. Some have allowed bitterness to grow and left the faith for an alternate identity. The world should never be able to offer people identity and a voice in a more powerful way than the *ekklesia*. He has given a voice and an invitation to all His people, once born again, to proclaim the good news of the gospel in all the earth. Again, Jesus is the answer to breaking the chains of identity confusion and has given us the ministry of reconciliation.

Thankfully, God draws all—men, women, and children—to Himself, and many, like myself, have turned their pain into humility and crazy faith through the seasons of rejection and silencing. The revelatory move of God is being birthed from hidden places. Thank the Lord for hidden mentors sent by the Father to His confused children. These special agents work to help these rejected ones turn their frustration into a lifestyle of prayer and fasting and personal reformation of the heart. Many who were confused are realizing that the silence the enemy meant for harm and confusion has awakened a heavenly voice that will soon be unleashed in the earthly realm. Now they are going out with boldness to reach the angry and broken in the world.

The truth is the humble will be exalted, and those who have endured and embraced the fiery trials are about to be unveiled and unleashed to blast a sound from heaven the world has never heard before (see Matt. 23:12). The people groups who have been oppressed will be transformed and emerge as holy glory carriers. They will become the forerunners of the awakening of the pure bride. These chosen, beautiful ones will find what it is to be not only sons and daughters, but also the beloved bride of their Bridegroom, Jesus Christ. They are even now realizing that who they are is who *He* is.

These are the ones we will see coming out of the wilderness places and waging war on oppression, and the identity crisis of the world, in the heavenly realms. From their prayer closets and prayer rooms, they have been going after breaking the chains of confusion in the LBGTQ community. They have developed the heart of God within them and have received prayers, songs, and messages from heaven that will lead to a massive harvest of souls among the very people the mainstream church system deemed unreachable.

Since 1999, nonstop live prayer and worship, including all nationalities and genders, has been happening in Kansas City, Missouri. The inclusion of all races, ages, and genders of people to pray and worship is the representation of the heavenly blueprint of every tribe, tongue, and nation declaring the worth of the Lamb. This phenomenon has birthed a movement of praying lovers of Jesus all over the earth. The platform of the preaching of human traditions and twisted interpretations of Scripture has been leveled, largely because of the movement to flip the tables, like Jesus did in the temple. The prayer movement, like Jesus, has made the house of God the Father's house of prayer again. This movement has birthed platforms of prayer and pure declaration of the Word of God. The ministry of reconciliation is taking place between God and people, and in people's relationships with one another, because the love of God flows in a culture of people who are making prayer and worship the focus of their lives.

As one move of God built upon another, the prayer room reconciliation led to The Call in 2000, 2007, and beyond. Through these events, a generation of Nazarites—John the Baptist-like consecrated ones, have committed to go beyond prayer houses and to live their lives as the answer to the prayers they have been praying. They have taken vows to be holy and set apart all the days of their lives. I am one of these modern Nazarites. It's amazing that prayer-and-revival branded lives have been birthed out of massive prayer meetings like The Call. From those prayer meetings, we went back to secret places all over the earth and planted houses of prayer in homes, dorm rooms, shopping centers, and wherever else we could meet with others to pray.

These events, focused on purely going after the face of God in fasting and prayer, have forever changed the DNA of those who attended. Though many of the minority groups listed earlier have felt frustrated about not having a place to share what they were seeing and hearing, they have learned to pray from a place of knowing God and knowing who they are rather than from a place of shame, frustration, or begging God. Even the oppression they experience in normal life has pressed them into deeper places of purity and encounter so they can lead many others to the way to freedom.

I believe masses of people have been transformed in this long period of hiddenness. In their desire to change the issues of the day while not being heard in the church, they have found freedom from their own issues. They are like the woman who suffered from internal haemorrhages who pressed her way through the unwelcoming crowd to secretly touch Jesus's prayer garment. Without realizing it, the hidden ones have received the virtue of Jesus and been healed. What they are beginning to realize now is that it was not about them, yet it was all about them. These burning, forgotten Nazarites and intercessors have been putting an end to the identity crisis in their own lives and changing the face of the earth with their prayers. They have given their lives to knowing God and being known by Him. They have been destroying racism, sexism, religious legalism, and the issues of the day in their own lives as they have cried out to God to end these issues in the world.

Are you one of these people? If not, do you want to be? These are the people who have been crying out with all they have, "Here am I, send me!" just like the prophet Isaiah (Is. 6:8). They do so because they want others to know the magnitude of Christ's beauty and holiness and the reward that comes with being set apart by His blood. The love and fire of the Spirit of God make us alive and wake us up to who we really are. If you have not yet experienced this, I invite you to stop right now and cry out to Jesus!

Many who have been burning on the inside and have gone through this process of personal refinement are beginning to see that they are the answer to their own prayers. They had to learn their identity first and learn that identity has nothing to do with what they do but is all about *whose* they are. The messages they carry have never been heard in the earth realm, besides in the written Word of God. Until now, the earth has not been ready for these messages. If you are one of these people, I want you to know that the silencing you have felt has not been in vain. Forgive the ignorant and receive healing from those wounds. You don't want to take that baggage with you.

Permission to Burn

The messages, songs, and prayers pulsing in your DNA are about to release deliverance and awakening like never before.

Awakening through the Daughters

The pastor's wife seemed to be depressed. Church members never really heard her speak from the platform unless there was a women's conference. What most didn't know at the time was that much of the leadership did not want women included in church decisions. Wives were welcome to sit with their husbands at the tables, but their input or discernment was not valued. He spent much of his time ministering to others but very little listening to his bride. His marriage eventually fell apart. She left him. She was involved in a homosexual relationship. His heart broke into a million pieces. Eyes were opened. He called the church together. He repented before them for his blindness. They fasted and prayed, and he ran after her. They both repented to one another, submitted to intense healing, and were restored. Now they minister together. Her voice is highly valued, and they are a force that hell can't stop.

I hear a sound coming from the depths of the souls of this company of people. They are beautifully adorned with the glory of the Father. They are His daughters and His sons—those who identify as His bride—His radiant ones. They were born to blow the trumpet and birth a movement. I prophesy to you today that these voices have been silenced for far too long. They have been choked out by religious and political fear and the twisting of the Scriptures, which makes this moment all the sweeter.

Freedom and reconciliation are the ministry of Jesus. The Bride is made up of every race and nationality—male and female, young and old. He loves to use what the world deems foolish to surprise those who think themselves the wisest in the political, religious, and worldly systems. Like Mary, the mother of Jesus, who "treasured all these things, pondering them in her heart" (Luke 2:19) after the angel visited her, these silenced voices have also pondered the unseen and unheard in their hearts, as they encounter heaven in prayer. They are no longer concerned with being validated by the religious systems. They have found validation in the Father. They have fallen in love with One whose throne is far above any earthly system.

I feel God saying to these,

> It was not a vain desire, to want to speak what you have seen and heard. It was not yet time to blow the trumpet. I was forming a movement in your spiritual wombs—a bridal revelation is soon to be birthed. I have been developing a countercultural purity in your messages. The next move of reconciliation with be between male and female in my body. Men who will bless female voices are stepping out of the shadows. They will be like Mordecais to my Esthers. Then the bridal movement will begin.

The time is now.

Reconciliation and Revelation through Sons and Daughters

The growing longing for the Bridegroom has caused many to weep and wail in dark corners and caves. They cry out for the dreams He has wrought in them to be born, yet we must see that He has hidden them as jewels for true reconciliation to be realized in its time, so the promise might come to birth. He is wielding an unspeakable gift in His bride's innermost being—dreams conceived in His daughters, only to be overlooked or deemed illegitimate in the name of religion. In the face of this, many women have left Christianity to go after the counterfeit feminist movement. As the tide begins to turn, women will find their true freedom and identity in Christ.

In this hour, God has placed a trumpet to the mouths of the women who were willing to draw close to His heart, just as He did for Mary and Elizabeth—He protected them even during times of religious shaming as they prepared to birth the long-awaited promises of the forerunner and Deliverer. He even silenced Zachariah for a season so that not one word that was not of the Lord would be spoken over Elizabeth's baby John. Like Elizabeth and Mary, many women have not rebelled against God in their pain but instead held tightly to the horns of the altar.

God has given these daughters secret heavenly revelation and wisdom; soon they will be released to shout it from rooftops (see Luke 12:3). Once the great company of daughters begins to speak, people—even those who think themselves wise—will recognize that these messages transcend human wisdom. "The Lord gives the command; the women who proclaim the good tidings are a great host" (Psalm 68:11). Restoration and reconciliation between the sons and daughters could be the greatest catalysts to culture transforming and awakening.

Mary knew she would birth something beyond her wildest dreams, and she pondered this in her heart (see Luke 2:19). For many years, women of every age and every race have longed to please their beloved Bridegroom. They have been willing to do whatever is necessary, even in silence, to bring His dwelling place and His presence to their homes, churches, and the earth. Revival history reveals how the Father used women and other minority groups to bring radical moves of His Spirit in previous generations because of their dedication to intercession.

Many today are content to believe that being hidden warriors is their mandate. However, something in them still groans to give birth and raise up the things they have ached and travailed for. These life bearers are full of wisdom and revelation, and they hold within them messages from heaven that will change the face of the earth. The Father longs to birth through them His image of perfect love, sacred bridal romance, and, ultimately, the bridal identity. We have heard the message of sonship—we are no longer orphans but children of God, but identifying as the bride of Christ has still been somewhat hidden and vaguely understood. Longing a bridal paradigm to be known is not limited to the daughters of God. For many years, amazing teachers like Mike Bickle (the founder of the International House of Prayer in Kansas City, MO) and others have plowed the trail in intercession and tears for the body of Christ to better understand this revelation. Soon, an unheard facet of the wonder of the Bridegroom will be released as women receive the blessing to sound the alarm. True sons of God are beginning to recognize that the righteous and pure identity of the church depends on the daughters coming out of hiding to teach, preach, and prophesy about the facets of His beauty that they ponder deep within their hearts.

A company of men is emerging that is protecting and promoting women now more than ever. Humanism wanted to destroy biblical family, but the Lord is putting it on display as He reconciles men and women in Himself. The unbridled flow of men and women ministering together will multiply the fruit of the gospel in the nations. Just as a man cannot conceive and bear a child alone, neither can he conceive, bear, and raise up the vision of heaven alone. Just as a woman cannot conceive and carry a child in her womb of her own accord, neither can she strengthen and grow this heavenly dream she carries alone once it is born.

Men of God, you have God's permission to arise and step into the bliss of reigning with and promoting the Lord's daughters. In the beginning, God said, "It is not good for the man to be alone" (Gen. 2:18). Adam was not capable of carrying out his commission to rule over the earth without Eve, nor was Eve capable without Adam. The same is true today. In His goodness, God created male and female to work together as one in the Spirit, just as the Father, Son, and Holy Spirit are one.

In 2015, I had an encounter with the Lord during which He spoke these words to me:

> In the same way that the Bridegroom, Jesus, was born from the womb of a woman, so will it be with the awakening of His love-sick bride in these last days. The first birth was the physical birth of Jesus into the world, but the second is a spiritual emergence of the global bridal identity.

This encounter revealed the Father's desire to impregnate His daughters with, and have them give birth to, His dream of the wonder of unity between Jesus the Bridegroom and His bride in the last days. Sons will begin to access levels of encounter, gripping intercession, and the wonder of the man Jesus in ways they never have before, as His daughters begin to ooze His glory.

This revelation reveals His plan to bring about the greater glory and the latter rain. Transformation will take place in the body of Christ that goes beyond the business of doing ministry and dives deeply into the beauty of *being* His ministry on the earth. Suddenly the church will experience the gripping of His love-sick longing for heart-to-heart connection with His bride.

Daughters are graced to carry the heavy glory of the bridal cry. His bride is His passion. The pure fire of His jealousy for her rages in His eyes. His sons are anointed with understanding of His jealous love and passion unto death. The convergence of these parts of revelation is a force hell can't stand against. We come a little closer to maturity in our knowing Him and knowing ourselves in Him. "For we know in part and we prophesy in part; but when the perfect comes the partial will be done away.... For now we see in a mirror dimly but then face to face; now I know in part but then I will know fully just as I am fully known" (1 Corinthians 13:9-10,12)

In this book, I am merely scratching the surface of this paradigm, or heavenly blueprint, of the bride and Bridegroom reigning as one. Truthfully, the revelation is not about gender but about Jesus and His unified church. So let us press forward through the elementary teachings, as Paul the apostle might say, and into the greater revelation. Consecration and unity between men and women of all nationalities and ages are essential to the coming move of God. As we allow this work to take place in the body of Christ, humanism-based identity confusion will be crushed.

As one, we will uproot the lies in the body so we can become the glorious bride. As the daughters of God gain permission to speak, we will hear and see our Father's kingdom message more clearly. The daughters of God were made to manifest a demand for consecration and passionate intimacy that demands a response from heaven.

Together, let us repent of the bondage we have walked in and be reconciled by His grace. Daughters of all ages, nationalities, and skin tones, you were born for such a time as this. You were created to be birthers of all the living. Birth the living Word and dreams of your Father in heaven. You were made to birth a revolution that manifests an identity of the church, which has long been overlooked and misunderstood. It's time for a bridal awakening!

I challenge you to declare aloud:

> This is Christ's longing, "that He might present to Himself the church in all her glory, having no spot or wrinkle or any such thing; but that she would be holy and blameless" (Eph. 5:27). Father, thank You for the grace to boldly walk out my part of revealing Your Son as the Bridegroom and the church as His bride.

14

From Permission to Ascension

For He has founded it upon the seas and established it upon the rivers. Who may ascend into the hill of the Lord? And who may stand in His holy place? He who has clean hands and a pure heart, who has not lifted up his soul to falsehood and has not sworn deceitfully. He shall receive a blessing from the Lord and righteousness from the God of his salvation. This is the generation of those who seek Him, who seek Your face—even Jacob. – Psalm 24:2–6

Permission to Burn

I wrote this book to stir longing in us to go after all the Father has placed in our hearts. I want to leave us longing for more of Him, and for the mystery of the One who longs to awaken His bride to be unveiled. "It is the glory of God to conceal a matter; to search out a matter is the glory of kings" (Prov. 25:2 NIV). In fact, permission granted is only the beginning. Permission is like saying you have been given grace to walk in a lifestyle of consecration and representation of Christ.

When a young man proposes to a young woman and she takes the ring and says yes, it is just the beginning of the dream of their lives together. He romances her and woos her. He gets her to the altar, and whether they realize it or not, this is just the beginning of their sacrifice and commitment to the new covenant between them and God. This altar experience is a whirlwind, what many call the best day of their lives. This is also often the case when we say I do to a life of fire and glory in relationship with Jesus.

He repeatedly gives us permission, but we repeatedly find ourselves seeking and searching for more. We have setbacks and failures. If we do not understand what we have been invited into, this process can cause us to feel rejected or abandoned as the days go on. When the journey gets hard and we find ourselves in the valleys, or in the ascent, we will war against the path He is leading us on. We must understand the true message of the cross and of grace. We can't burn for Him without Him.

David understood this reality when he wrote: "Even though I walk through the valley of the shadow of death, I fear no evil, for You are with me" (Ps. 23:4). This psalm is often read at funerals, but David never meant this to be so somber or to say the valley of the shadow of death is a negative thing. This valley is a place of fearlessness and of

From Permission to Ascension

supernaturally relying on God to cover and shoulder the load. It is time of knowing the Psalm-91 experience of dwelling in the shadow of the Almighty. In this dwelling place, fear is no more. Though one thousand may fall at our side and ten thousand at our right hand, it will not come near the dwelling place of God's shadow. God is perfect love, and His shadow covers us in costly grace. "There is no fear in love; but perfect love casts out fear; because fear involves punishment; and the one who fears has not been perfected in love" (1 John 4:18).

When we are in the valley, we often forget whose shadow we dwell in, and we step into fear. If we aren't careful, we will step into legalism and depend on our own works to be our resting place. In response, God challenges us to ascend again to the place where we are seated with Him—at the right hand of the Father. A good study on where He is positioned eternally will help you understand your heavenly position. The key is not as much about where we sit, but *who* we sit with (Acts 7:55-56; Rom. 8:34; Eph. 1:20, 2:6; Col. 3:1; Heb. 8:1). Without this understanding, burnout is inevitable.

I focused on my own righteousness before I grasped my position is not to work from earth to heaven but from heaven to earth. You are working with and through Him by His grace. If you do not rightly apply grace, you will eventually become trapped in depression and anxiety. You will feel as though you are never good enough. *Father, forgive me. I hurt another person. Father, my thoughts are not pure. I yelled today. I got angry. Did I spend enough time reading the Scriptures? Praying? Oh, God, I'm not good enough to be a messenger for you.* Day in and day out, this is the prayer life of a woman who has forgotten she has permission to need His grace. In my pursuit of holiness and burning, I began living under the pressure of my own expectations. By nature, I am a perfectionist. I was striving, pressing toward holiness in my own strength. Now I never want to abuse His grace.

I had made inner vows that I would never preach that "hyper-grace" message or allow lawlessness, because as a reformer, I want truth to be shouted from the rooftops. Though this sounds like a good goal to have, I had no idea that I personally had come under the heavy burden of legalism. Like the Galatians, I forgot Jesus called me while I was still a sinner and the work was by His Spirit, not my own flesh. I had taken a heavy burden on my shoulders. "You foolish Galatians! Who has bewitched you? Before your very eyes Jesus Christ was clearly portrayed as crucified. . . . Did you receive the Spirit by the works of the law, or by believing what you heard? Are you so foolish? After beginning by means of the Spirit, are you now trying to finish by means of the flesh?" (Galatians 3:1-3). In my war against lawlessness, I had actually lost sight of the biblical message of grace. I had repentance down. I did it day and night, but I didn't receive His grace, and I needed it to walk in joy. I wanted nothing more than to please Him.

If we begin to look at our sin more than we look at His wonder, we will remove our robes of righteousness and return to trying to clean up our filthy rags (Is. 61:10; 64:6). My flame was dwindling. The Lord tenderly spoke to me as I wept. *You come to me repenting all day long of things I have chosen to forget. I called you when you were still a sinner, and you rejoiced over my grace and love. Now you are trying to earn favor with me by your works. I called you to come boldly to the throne of grace and ask of me for the nations, but you come in fear and unworthiness, only focused on the dirt covering your feet. Look at*

From Permission to Ascension

me. Sit with me. Let me wash your feet. Let me remove the heavy yoke. Let's do this work together. You can't burn without my grace. Take off your own righteousness and wear mine again.

The place of ascent is for the believer living in the born-again covenant with Jesus (because of His blood) and is filled with His Spirit (because of His promise). This is simply a reminder of our position in His kingdom. This glorious ascent is more than a journey of circumstances; it is about learning to live where we were created to live—with Him in heavenly places, even while we are living here on earth.

The idea of being in the world but not of it is a deeper revelation than we might think. It is a call to come up higher and to live seated in the place Jesus ascended to, working with a heavenly perspective that is greater than just having a mansion one day when we pass from this earth. Maybe this is an invitation to go where David only dared to dream of. "One thing I have asked from the Lord, that I shall seek: that I may dwell in the house of the Lord all the days of my life, to behold the beauty of the Lord and to meditate in His temple" (Ps. 27:4).

This is not a place of striving to be good or do things. It is a place where we find our dwelling in Him—the home Jesus died to give us. We find our home with Him all the days of our lives and live in the place of seeking and knowing Him daily. We ascend the hill of the Lord even when we are in the valley; we are going after clean hands and a pure heart as we journey in deeper devotion. In this we can truly see Him with spiritual eyes and know Him deeply. This ascent is a place of awakening the heart and mind—to things beyond the physical realm of striving into holy thriving. Jesus said, in His Sermon on the Mount, "Blessed are the pure in heart, for they shall see God"

(Matt. 5:8). I believe He was referring to the pure heart David wrote about, "Who may ascend the mountain of the Lord? Who may stand in his holy place? The one who has clean hands and a pure heart" (Ps. 24:3-4). A heart transforms into purity when we spend more time gazing at His wonder and marvelling over His perfection than analyzing our own shortcomings. We change because we are amazed.

David wrote this psalm as he was ascending the mountain to establish the dwelling place of the Lord, the ark of the covenant. He was doing this after the previous king, Saul, had defiled the land with idolatry and removed the presence of God from Israel. David established what he saw in heaven as he chased the heart of God. He established what he learned from Moses, who set up the tent of meeting in the wilderness, so he set up day-and-night prayer, worship, and declaration of the Scriptures. Even more than that, he set up a place where all could come and encounter the presence of the one true God. He knew that working to clean up the mess Saul made began with enthroning the presence of God. Without engaging the culture in the beauty of the majesty of the Lord, everything else would be in vain. He made it clear that repentance of the nation was necessary, and clean hands and pure hearts were required to ascend that hill. David, "the man after God's own heart," led the charge by example as he danced and humbly removed his prideful kingly garments and assumed the humble garments of priestly service (see 2 Samuel 6:14).

Jesus represented and echoed this purity as He sat on the mount and declared the Beatitudes, yet what He promised was even greater than what those listening could imagine. Jesus spoke of something coming greater than

From Permission to Ascension

Moses's tent or David's tent—He said the pure in heart wouldn't just go on the mountain to pray. He said He would very soon make a way for all to receive the purity He provides.

This is a calling higher than just worship on a mountain. This is about ascending to the place where eye has not seen and ear has not heard, a place where people can see God with pure hearts. The journey to Golgotha that Jesus made proved that a pure heart is the pathway to being seated at the right hand of the Father in the days to come. Jesus demonstrated that the place of God's beauty and presence would not be contained in buildings but in the hearts of people. He became the example of a greater place of worship, and then He gifted it to "whosoever will."

This ascent into dwelling with God paves the way to all the promises contained in the canonized Scriptures. However, the requirements are just the same: purity, love, God's love in us, and grace, which empower us to live it. Lawlessness will never do. Only from the place of relationship can we find our way to a pure heart that sees God.

So many people think the Amos 9:11 prophecy of the rebuilding of David's fallen tent is about a physical place on the dirt on the earth. This could be true. I'm not a master theologian, but I believe it's greater than that. I believe "God with us" looks like us being His tent of meeting, in which our hearts are the altar and He has our constant gaze. This altar that is ours must burn day and night with the fire of purity as we sacrifice our limited human will, emotions, and mind to take up the will of God, the mind of Christ, and the emotions of His heart. I do believe God is establishing physical places of day-and-night worship, prayer, and declaration of His Word all over the earth, and Amos 9:11 will be established this way as well.

But I know with every fiber of my being that His dream is for His bride to arise and for His breath to be released through her. As she comes together desiring just one thing—to live in His presence and gaze upon His beauty all the days of her life—we will begin to see the fivefold ministry we so often talk about established through lifestyles of intercession and worship. As we live this way, we will realize that the message is not one of holiness or grace but of the grace to be holy. Then the bride without spot or blemish will arise from the ashes, and the church—the *ekklesia* of the last days—will be vigorous, even if the world around her is shaking. She will be glorious! The gates of hell do not stand a chance.

Awakening and Commission

Not long after my experience at The Call Nashville in 2007, God shifted our entire family from being subdued into being free again. God, through His Son, my Bridegroom, gave me that permission; and permission thrust me into His boldness. I was marked by a holy hunger that thrust me into a lifestyle of ascending, of learning the beauty of abiding in Him, of walking out the Great Commission. Beloved, I haven't finished my race, nor have you. The journey is wild and full of adventure. Offence will come. Bleed love. Let us not just begin well but finish well. Knowing who we are and how to sustain the holy inferno as His chosen messenger is imperative. God has created you to be a firebrand, to live a lifestyle that breaks the chains of lawless compromise, and to live as a holy generation.

From Permission to Ascension

Don't ever forget that the burning is sustained by abiding in Him by His grace, not by striving. We are His "chosen people, a royal priesthood, a holy nation, God's special possession, so that you may proclaim the excellencies of Him who called you out of the darkness into His marvelous light" (1 Peter 2:9). No matter what comes, we have been sealed with something greater than what the world has to offer. This earth is not our home—not now, and not when our bodies are laid to rest. We are sojourners here on a mission, together. Our mission begins with receiving the permission to live holy, pure, fiery lives, but it doesn't end there! We were created to bring awakening to the burning hearts of His people. We were born for this. At the final trumpet sound, we, His bride, will meet Him in the sky. May our declaration be, "We have overcome by the blood of the Lamb and the word of our testimony." In the words of the Moravians, "May the Lamb receive the reward of His suffering."

May you be a sign and a wonder, a burning bush, and a vessel of His presence all the days of your life. In light of that, let's declare this together by the power of His Spirit.

I have permission to be holy.

I have permission to burn.

I have permission to declare His Word and to be pure.

I have permission to do it the way the Bible says to do it, with His grace to empower me.

I have permission to do everything that is written and breathed by His breath in the Scriptures. I fear no man!

I have permission to burn.

PERMISSION TO BURN

Dear burning one,

> Permission granted.

PERMISSION TO SPEAK.

PERMISSION TO DREAM.

PERMISSION TO BURN.

PERMISSION GRANTED.

PERMISSION TO UNIFY WITH THE BURNING HEARTS OF THOSE AROUND YOU.

PERMISSION TO SAY NO TO BEING SUBDUED BY HUMAN WAYS AND THE FEAR OF PEOPLE'S OPINIONS.

PERMISSION TO LOVE INTO FREEDOM THE ONES BOUND IN RELIGION AND THE ONES DECEIVED BY LAWLESSNESS.

PERMISSION TO LOVE THE ONES WHO HATE YOU.

> Continue to burn.
> My question is, are you ready?
> Burn, beloved, burn! I am praying for you.
>> Heal the sick, raise the dead, cleanse those who have leprosy, drive out demons. Freely you have received; freely give. . . . Then the eleven disciples went to Galilee, to the mountain where Jesus had told them to go. When they saw him, they worshiped him; but some doubted. Then Jesus came to them and said, "All authority in heaven and on earth has been given to me. Therefore go and make disciples of all nations, baptizing them in

From Permission to Ascension

the name of the Father and of the Son and of the Holy Spirit, and teaching them to obey everything I have commanded you. And surely I am with you always, to the very end of the age."

– Matthew 10:8; 28:16-20 NIV

Works Cited

Chapter 2

Paul McRae, "Paul McRae Testimony Summer Intensive 2016" (in author's possession).

Chapter 5

Pia Jo Reynolds, "Pia Reynolds MS Fire" (in author's possession).

Chapter 6

Tony Ramos, "A House of Prayer for All Nations" (in author's possession).

Chapter 8

Jessica Southerland, "Permission" (in author's possession).

Alan Doyle, "Permission to Burn Statement" (in author's possession).

Chapter 9

Lou Engle, "Pray! Ekballo! A Prayer Revolution for the Great Harvest," Mission Frontiers, Jul/Aug 2014, accessed October 2, 2018, https://www.missionfrontiers.org/pdfs/36-4-Ekballo.pdf.ia Jo Reynolds, "Pia Reynolds MS Fire" (in author's possession).

Chapter 11

Merriam-Webster.com, s.v. "humanism."

Chapter 13

Lou Engle, "God Is Calling Us to Fasting and Prayer—and to Answer the Call on 7-07-07 in Nashville and Where You Live!" The Elijah List (March 19, 2007); http://www.elijahlist.com/words/display_word/5107 (accessed August 22, 2018).

Appendix A

The Context of 1 Corinthians 14:34

Because this verse has so frequently been abused, it is important to briefly explain the context of Paul's statement, so we can position our hearts toward true reconciliation and put to death the division among us. The law Paul referred to here is the man-made law of the Pharisees, which was being taught among the Corinthians; however, Jesus abolished this law, as stated in Galatians 3 (which Paul also wrote).

In 1 Corinthians 14:34, Paul was responding with sarcasm to the double-mindedness of the Corinthian converts when he said, "Women should be silent in the churches." This is something he often did in his letters. We know Paul was being sarcastic because of the context of the letter. The book of 1 Corinthians is one of Paul's letters to the church of Corinth, in which he addressed questions they had asked him in a previous letter (which is lost to history). The Corinthians were coming out of paganism and being exposed to religious teachings from the Jews, and as a result, they were very confused.

The proof of Paul's sarcasm about women speaking in church is evident in the verses just prior.

> For you can all prophesy one by one, *so that all may learn and all may be exhorted;* and the spirits of prophets are subject to prophets; for God is not a God of confusion but of peace, as in all the churches of the saints.
>
> – 1 Corinthians 14:31–33, emphasis mine

The statement "women should be silent" is not congruent with "You can all prophesy." It is like Paul was saying, "You asked about whether or not women should be silent. That's a crazy question! Why are you referring again to the law? Was it from you that the word of God first went forth, or has it come to you only? I just said all may prophesy; just do it in decency and in order so there's no confusion" (my paraphrase of 1 Corinthians 14:36).

When we read these verses in context, we find that Paul was encouraging all to prophesy and speak in tongues. He didn't want to silence anyone but to establish order. He was telling them to stop reverting back to human tradition and law and reminding them of their freedom in Christ to be one.

This verse has been taken out of historical and scriptural context for far too long and has been used to enslave women to silence. No more!

Appendix B

Sons and Daughters of God

Because the word "sonship" has the potential to cause confusion, I felt it necessary to explain the context behind this word. Ephesians 5:1-3 uses the metaphor of adoption to express how the blood of Jesus transforms the identity of the believer. It moves us from orphaned sinners who were once separated from God to righteous ones, whom He refers to as His very own adopted sons. This is not gender specific. Some translations use "children" rather than "sons," but I do not believe that the use of the word sons is at all faulty. I believe it to be a spiritual concept, in the same way that Galatians 3:28 uses the word sons to refer to "the bride of Christ" and the "body of Christ."

The New Testament often uses metaphors to express different aspects of life in Christ. Simply put, it is clear that in Christ we are no longer identified by the life we once lived in the flesh. Therefore, we rise above this gender issue and go deeper by identifying ourselves as His very own sons and daughters, who by the blood of Jesus, realize we are made in His image and His likeness. We are no longer merely male or female, fleshly beings. Sonship or daughterhood is a part of our lifestyle as children of God. "We are joint-heirs with Christ and our identity is consumed in Him. All male and female alike who accept the atoning sacrifice of Jesus Christ are sons through faith in Him" (Rom. 8:16-17).

> All of you who were baptized into Christ have clothed yourselves with Christ. There is neither Jew nor Greek, slave nor free, male nor female, for you are all one in Christ Jesus. And if you belong to

Christ, then you are Abraham's seed and heirs according to the promise. . . . male nor female.

– Galatians 3:28; Romans 8:16-17; 9:24; Ephesians 5:1-3

Acknowledgments

Editing and Book-Birthing Team

(Because writing a book is like birthing a baby)

Angie Woodard: Transcriptionist, developmental editor, and copyeditor (the midwife).

Amy Caulkins: Developmental editor (the doctor).

Sally Hanan: Copyeditor, proofreader, and typesetter (the surgeon).

Brian Francis Hume: Intercessor, encourager, connector, and publishing expert (the labor coach).

The Kid Wranglers and Homestead Helpers

(Because writing a book while being a minister and mom of three littles is like birthing a fourth baby.)

Crystal Hornbeck: The "older sister" and homestead mess wrangler.

Daymon Southerland: My amazing husband, blessed provider, and father of the wild-girl gang.

The Wild Girl Gang

My daughters, Eden, Jayden, and Aldey Southerland: The inspiration and passion stokers who gave me the push to get this message out so that my ceiling will be your floor.

My Parents and Brother

Phillip and Debbie Fortner: For telling me I can do anything I can put my mind to.

Brian Fortner: Just because you're awesome.

Book Cover Art

Darrian and Amanda Shiflett: Life Designs and Media.

The Many Hidden Intercessors

Your names and rewards remain known in heaven. You prayed through the delays, blocks, and walls.

I thank you all. I could not have done this without you!

About Tammie

Tammie Southerland pioneered and serves as the forerunning leader of Frontline Ministries International, a long-time mobile prayer and equipping ministry that now serves as an umbrella for others all across the nation who desire to live a lifestyle of holiness and passion for Jesus. FLM was founded on prayer for the purpose of equipping, training, and launching people into their God-given destinies. She leads the south-eastern region for Awaken the Dawn, is an executive leader and messenger for Sealed 2020, and travels throughout the United States as a guest speaker.

She is also the founder and apostolic leader for The Firehouse Prayer Furnace in Seneca, SC. She is covered by the International House of Prayer in Atlanta, GA. As a gifted teacher, prophet, and lightning rod for revival, she is igniting a generation to burn with passion for Jesus. Her heart beats for the people of God to enjoy the beauty of His presence daily.

At the time of this writing, Tammie and her husband, Daymon, reside in South Carolina with their three children.

Connect with Tammie

Website: www.tammiesoutherland.org

YouTube: FrontLine Ministries and/or Tammie Southerland

Facebook: facebook.com/tammiesoutherland

Share your thoughts: tammie@frontlinefire.org

Book Tammie to speak: booking@frontlinefire.org

CAN YOU HELP?

Reviews are everything to an author, because they mean a book is given more visibility. If you enjoyed this book, please review it on your favorite book review sites and tell your friends about it. Thank you!

www.ingramcontent.com/pod-product-compliance
Lightning Source LLC
Chambersburg PA
CBHW052025070526
44584CB00016B/1910